The Appraisal of Religions Facilities

Readers of this text may be interested in the following books from the Appraisal Institute:
The Appraisal of Real Estate, eleventh edition; and *Historic Properties: Preservation and the Valuation Process,* second edition, by Judith Reynolds, MAI.

For a catalog of Appraisal Institute publications, contact the PR/Marketing Department of the Appraisal Institute, 875 N. Michigan Ave., Ste. 2400, Chicago, Illinois 60611-1980.

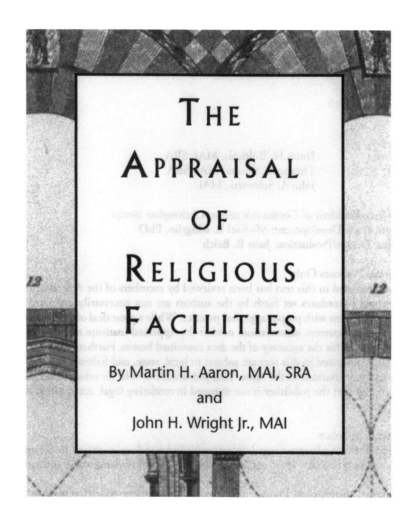

THE
APPRAISAL
OF
RELIGIOUS
FACILITIES

By Martin H. Aaron, MAI, SRA
and
John H. Wright Jr., MAI

**APPRAISAL
INSTITUTE**®

875 NORTH MICHIGAN AVENUE
CHICAGO, ILLINOIS 60611-1980

Reviewers: James H. Bulthuis, MAI, SRA
              Thomas A. Motta, MAI, SRA
              John A. Schwartz, MAI

Senior Vice President of Communications: Christopher Bettin
Manager, Book Development: Michael R. Milgrim, PhD
Manager, Design/Production: Julie B. Beich

Printed in the United States of America

Library of Congress Cataloging-in-Publication Data
Aaron, Martin H.
    The appraisal of religious facilities / by Martin H. Aaron and John H. Wright, Jr.
        p.   cm.
    ISBN 0-922154-39-2
    1. Religious facilities—Valuation—United States.   I. Wright, John H., 1960-
II. Title.
BL2525.A23   1997   97-19783
333.33'87—dc21   CIP

Table of Contents

Foreword

Over the years the Appraisal Institute has published a number of titles pertaining to special-use or special-purpose properties. We are now pleased to add religious facilities to that list. The appraisal of a religious facility is not an everyday assignment. Because of the unique physical attributes common to many of these facilities as well as specialized markets, these properties require particular insights and knowledge on the part of the appraiser.

As *The Appraisal of Religious Facilities* points out, today's religious facility may be a 100-year-old edifice with towering ceilings and steeples or a modern "campus-like" facility that offers not only space for worship but social and community events as well. Property use as well as physical design therefore are important elements in assessing value.

The Appraisal Institute is pleased to publish *The Appraisal of Religious Facilities*. It is our hope that this book will inform and guide appraisers in this specialized area of property valuation.

Kenneth L. Nicholson, SRA
1997 President
Appraisal Institute

Acknowledgments

First and foremost we must thank our wives, Dorit H. Aaron and Donna N. Wright, for allowing us the time to develop this work outside of our regular and busy work schedules. Secondly we wish to thank our children, Margo and Haley Aaron and Hunter, Elizabeth, and Harrison Wright, for being patient with us when we said we couldn't be around because we had to work on "the book."

From a professional standpoint we wish to thank all of the competent religious facility lenders, appraisers, reviewers, bankers, architects, builders, and others who not only gave us insight but also a reason to doubt. This led us to "keep digging" and to investigate more fully numerous issues that went into this text.

Last but not least we wish to thank our complete staff of professionals who have been hearing about "the book" for a long time and whose support, hard work, and dedication helped to give us the insight to write this text.

Martin H. Aaron, MAI, SRA
John H. Wright Jr., MAI

August 1997

About the Authors

Martin H. Aaron, MAI, SRA, and John H. Wright Jr., MAI, are principals in the firm of Aaron & Wright and Aaron & Wright Technical Services. Aaron & Wright is a full-service real estate appraisal firm specializing in the valuation of religious facilities and assets for securitized and agency transactions. The firm has offices in Boston, Philadelphia, Chicago, Houston, and Newport Beach. Aaron & Wright Technical Services provides environmental site assessments and property condition assessments to a variety of clients throughout the United States.

Messrs. Aaron and Wright are extremely active nationally in valuing religious facilities, having appraised facilities ranging from a modified pole barn to $100 million complexes. A forerunner of this book was published as an article entitled "The Valuation of Religious Facilities" in the January 1992 issue of *The Appraisal Journal.*

Martin H. Aaron has over 21 years of appraisal experience. He appraised his first religious facility in 1978, and through his extensive experience, he has developed a standard methodology for the valuation of this type of facility. Under his direction, the firm has valued numerous religious facilities for a variety of clients and purposes including purchase, sale, financing, foreclosure, and bankruptcy. Aaron has served as an expert witness in both civil and bankruptcy courts on numerous occasions. He also is a licensed general contractor/contract developer. He holds a bachelor of science degree in business administration, with majors in real estate and finance, from the University of Missouri at Columbia.

John H. Wright Jr. has been an appraiser since 1983, and his background also includes functioning as the regional manager of a super regional bank. Along with being a seasoned appraiser of religious facilities, Wright has an extensive background in the valuation of income properties. In addition to coauthoring this text, Wright has written numerous articles on reviewing appraisals and other aspects of real estate valuation. He is a member of the Mortgage Bankers Association and is active in the mortgage-backed securities industry. Wright holds a degree in business administration from South Texas State University.

The authors formed the firm of Aaron & Wright, Inc., which has grown into one of the largest appraisal firms in the country.

Chapter One
INTRODUCTION: WHY VALUE RELIGIOUS PROPERTIES?

Most often the valuation of a religious facility relates to financing. A religious group may be adding to an existing facility, proposing to build a new one, or buying a used facility. Numerous variations of these possibilities exist. Sometimes the valuation is related to a failed or foreclosed facility. As groups grow or decline, they often need to know the value of their facility to make decisions relative to their congregations' needs. Religious groups also may need to ascertain the reasonableness of an asking price or an offer to purchase. Most ruling bodies have a fiduciary responsibility to their members to determine if an offer or listing price is reasonable. Value also is an important issue for insurance purposes, especially for older facilities or ones that contain antiquities or have historical significance. Insurance companies appear reluctant to provide *reproduction cost* insurance for such facilities; rather, their *replacement cost* becomes the benchmark for insurance purposes, as will be discussed in detail in this book.

On some occasions, an existing congregation will want to disband or form two or more separate congregations. This often requires the valuation of a portion of the facility and/or a fractional or partial interest to determine how the values are segmented or how the properties could be split up. In some cases, buyers only want a portion of the facility or want to "share it" with another group.

Valuation of religious facilities generally consists of either *market value* or *value in use.* Market value is generally synonymous with value in exchange according to most definitions. It is often defined as what a typical buyer would pay for a property, given a reasonable marketing period. The marketing period can be extensive depending on the activity level in the market as well as the type and location of the facility.

Some lenders are willing to use a value-in-use premise in underwriting loans to religious groups. *The Dictionary of Real Estate Appraisal*[1] defines value in use as "the value a

---

1 Appraisal Institute, *The Dictionary of Real Estate Appraisal,* third edition (Chicago: Appraisal Institute, 1993).

specific property has for a specific use." It is a legitimate valuation methodology with respect to special-use properties. Value in use implies a value to a particular user, which in the case of religious properties may or may not be the congregation in place. A basic assumption of the value-in-use premise is that the congregation in question can afford the existing or proposed facility. Obviously, a particular congregation's needs could differ significantly from the "market norm." There are numerous cases where a particular facility is significantly more valuable to one owner or user than another. For example, one group may need a large sanctuary because its focus is preaching whereas another group whose focus is education might prize a facility with a larger percentage of classroom space. For some congregations, a facility without a baptistery is useless, and for other congregations, the baptistery must face a certain direction. The value-in-use concept is supported by the fact that religious groups often will decide to build new, rather than buy at a depreciated cost figure or discount a facility that is not exactly what they need. Value in use is particularly applicable when a facility completely fulfills the specific needs of the congregation.

Obviously, a religious group needs to know the value of land that it plans to purchase for expansion and/or new construction. On some occasions and in some municipalities, religious facilities are taxed on their vacant land. The trend appears to be growing for local municipalities to levy ad valorem taxes on nonprofit groups.

As religious bodies have become more and more involved in the day-to-day lives of their members, their facilities have become significantly more complex and expensive. In the United States there are now some facilities that cost in excess of $100 million. As such, their physical operation and fiscal administration are important issues. Additionally, their valuation issues have also become more complex.

This book will outline the basis from which value permeates in religious facilities. Chapters 2 and 3 provide an overview of the development of religious facilities in the United States. Chapter 2 offers a historical perspective on the evolution of religious facilities, and Chapter 3 discusses the marketplace for religious facilities and its relationship to value. Chapter 4 focuses on the physical facility. As religious facilities are special-use properties, this chapter will provide a reference point for describing most facilities. Chapter 5 looks at land value, which examines zoning, highest and best use issues, use permits, schools, alternative uses, and other land issues.

Applications of the cost approach and sales comparison approach are presented in Chapters 6 and 7. Items discussed in Chapter 6 include sources of support for cost new, estimation of depreciation using the extraction or sales comparison approach and breakdown methods of developing total depreciation, functional and external depreciation, and separation of land and building. The chapter also presents a discussion on the ramifications of the cost approach on the balance of the report. In Chapter 7 comparables and their sources will be discussed along with suggested methodologies for analyzing diverse data, including a case study showing the application of the sales comparison approach.

The book concludes with a chapter on financing religious facilities, which focuses on feasibility from a lender's perspective. Loan sources, typical underwriting requirements, and income characteristics are discussed. Some lenders currently maintain that lending to a religious group has little to do with the real estate, but that a "credit analysis" or cash flow (analysis) should be the primary collateral for the loan. Obviously, appraisers doubt the assumption that the total validity of a loan secured in part by real estate could or should be made strictly on the basis of cash flow, but nonetheless, this is a current issue, and it is discussed in this book.

The purpose of this book is to provide the reader with a reasonable amount of background in order to understand the valuation process relative to religious facilities and to properly and reasonably estimate their value. As such, this book is intended for professional appraisers, architects, brokers, lenders, religious facility administrators/business managers, contractors, and others involved with religious facilities so that they can more fully understand the source from which value permeates in religious facilities.

A final comment: The emphasis of this book is on "religious facilities" be they churches, synagogues, temples, mosques, or other worship structures. However, it is recognized that the percentage of Christian churches in the United States far exceeds that of other types of houses of worship, and therefore churches represent the largest pool of possible appraisal assignments. While some of the descriptions and examples in this book reflect the preponderance of churches, the techniques presented are presumed applicable to any house of worship regardless of the faith or beliefs of the religious body involved.

Appraisers are reminded that the same standards of professional appraisal practice that apply to the valuation of any other type of property also pertain to the appraisal of a religious facility. To that end, in assessing potential markets, the characteristic of "religion" must be used very carefully in reaching any conclusion of value. Appraisers should be knowledgeable about applicable federal, state, and local laws that affect the subject property of an assignment, and must provide appraisals that do not illegally discriminate or contribute to illegal discrimination. The Ethics Provision of the Uniform Standards of Professional Appraisal Practice (USPAP) states that an appraiser cannot rely on unsupported conclusions relating to certain characteristics, including religion, and further that an appraiser cannot rely on an unsupported conclusion that homogeneity of such characteristics is necessary to maximize value.

Appraisers are directed to review USPAP's Advisory Opinion 16, "Fair Housing Laws and Appraisal Report Content," which also stresses the importance of not relying on unsupported conclusions. Among the examples cited in AO-16 to illustrate issues surrounding this topic is that of the appraisal of a religious facility. While AO-16 concludes that such an assignment is not covered by the Fair Housing Act or the Equal Credit Opportunity Act, the key to the assignment is not to rely on unsupported conclusions. "If the appraiser can identify the market behavior of the religious members and relate that behavior to the assignment, the appraiser is not in violation of USPAP."

Chapter Two
HISTORICAL PERSPECTIVE OF RELIGIOUS FACILITIES

This book is not about religion but about the places in which people practice their religion. The development of religious facilities in the United States has generally paralleled the needs of its communities as they spread across the country. In the early years religious facilities typically acted as meeting or gathering places for the community in addition to serving as places of worship. At times a facility may have served as a school or classroom, voting hall, and community center. The house of worship was a focal point where many important decisions of the community were made.

A typical facility was built to seat most of the active community at a given time and consisted mostly of a sanctuary (or worship space). In those days, a facility that could not seat most of the members at one time was marginally adequate. This has remained true today. The primary function of the facility was obviously for worship services, but a facility that could not also double as a school or meeting room or for some other multiple purpose use was considered only nominally adequate.

By the early 1900s, some very large and ornate facilities had been built in many communities; these buildings, however, still focused primarily on the sanctuary. From an appraiser's perspective, these structures are among the most challenging in today's market. Numerous older facilities exist with functional superadequacies such as overly high ceilings, very thick exterior walls, or extremely ornate designs. Obviously, in today's market, these exceed typical construction quality. Buildings with large sanctuaries, ornate stained glass, high ceilings, granite exteriors, steeples, and bell towers are intriguing from an aesthetic, architectural, and/or historic standpoint, but they may have reduced function based on today's requirements. The challenge of reproduction cost versus replacement cost with facilities such as these is a major issue with insurance groups.

Religious facilities have evolved based on the needs of individual congregations or particular religious groups. For example, some religious groups focus on preaching, praying, ceremonial bathing/washing (thus the need for pools or tubs), teaching, feeding the hungry (thus the need for kitchens), and carrying out other philanthropic endeavors

Located in a downtown (CBD) area, this church is representative of the often ornate and intricate facilities built in the United States in the late 19th and early 20th centuries. In many cases they are not functional in the modern environment (parking, seating, etc.) and represent some of the most complex valuation issues.

that expanded religious facilities. Typical in this evolution was the development of schools/classrooms, administrative offices, kitchens, and even retail sales areas (e.g., book stores), along with a more comfortable environment in which to worship.

With the growth of suburbia after World War II, religious facilities sprouted up supporting the post-war growth of new homes. Many of these facilities were typically red brick structures with steeples and large sanctuaries and were designed primarily for one or two weekly services. A ratio 10 square feet of seating area to 30 square feet of total building area was typical. As administrative areas, classrooms, kitchens, libraries, living quarters, and other areas were added, these ratios expanded. Over the next 30 years facilities grew and amenities were added, fulfilling not only the needs of the religious group but also the needs of the general community.

Some newer facilities have a campus-like setting with numerous peripheral buildings. Generally such buildings are carefully added as needed; they may be connected or adjacent to the existing facility or marginally distant from it. There appears to be a relationship between a congregation's propensity to exist in or nearby its current location and the likelihood of the group's expanding to noncontiguous sites or even sites several miles away in order to more fully serve its members.

Many campus settings exist where each building fulfills a different need. Sanctuary,

The functional design of this structure is typical of many newer religious facilities found more often in suburban and outlying areas. Its principal features are a center sanctuary, with a balcony, and two two-story classroom/administrative wings for support activities. Adequate parking is also present.

administrative offices, school/classrooms, and day-care facilities may be in different buildings connected by a series of covered walks. Numerous other variations on the "campus" concept have evolved. These include adding to an existing sanctuary (typically a very big job) or adding classrooms, administrative offices, choir rooms, gyms, multipurpose rooms, and living quarters. In most cases these additions tend to function well with the existing facility so that functional obsolescence is not present. The lack of functional obsolescence in many religious facilities is due to the careful planning of additions, coupled with the size of the additions. Many times the addition becomes the focal point of the facility, making the original facility secondary to the addition. Examples of functional obsolescence will be discussed later in this book.

A campus type of facility usually requires land for expansion, which has prompted some urban groups to move to the suburbs. Generally, urban facilities are older and the areas around them are built up. Thus, little land is available for expansion and the buildings that are needed by the congregation cannot be built in its existing location. Many times the older building is sold and the congregation moves to a more suburban location where land is available. These moves parallel the demographic move toward suburban communities, which is evident in virtually every city and town in the country. Typically an existing urban facility then may be acquired by a new and sometimes ethnic congregation.

Urban facilities in built-up areas as well as newer campus-like settings are a function of the needs that were present at the time growth occurred or is needed. That is to say, a facility may last well over 100 years physically, but the needs of the community may change so that the facility simply does not fulfill the needs of its members.

Among trends affecting the development of religious facilities today include the public schools crisis, the demand for day-care centers, and caring for the elderly. The deterioration of public schools (or perception thereof) throughout much of the nation has caused the populace to ask their religious leaders to fulfill the education function. Thus, many newer facilities have desired to build a school or add on to an existing school. With more working mothers, day-care facilities are becoming prevalent. Religious institutions are also being asked to help in caring for our aging population. All of these situations are relatively recent compared to the age of our existing stock of religious facilities. "Older" facilities (some only a few years old) are unable to support their congregations adequately based on the above types of demands.

A more recent phenomenon—which will likely exist for many years—in the development of religious structures is the addition of "family life centers." These multipurpose rooms/buildings typically provide large halls designed for any number of activities. Typically, the area can double as a gym, dining hall, party room, secondary sanctuary, youth room, or theater. The concept is to have a space where the congregation can conduct more ancillary activities. Such centers are often built around classrooms, administrative offices, or other more typical uses. These additions will likely provide "flex space" for religious facilities for many years to come.

Another recent phenomenon is the growth of television ministries and educational programs. Some facilities need a structure in which to videotape and/or audiorecord, broadcast, edit, and store programs. These functions require extensive electrical service, coaxial cables, fiber optics, etc. Many religious groups that actively proselytize (that is, recruit new members) require media-oriented rooms/sections. Some groups own and operate their own radio stations directly from their facilities.

Acoustics can be a major issue. Many facilities that were built before adequate public address systems became the norm have excellent acoustics. Others, built without the attention to acoustics, remain obsolete from that standpoint even with today's advanced PA systems. Numerous facilities exist that were built without any attention to acoustics. In an attempt to improve the acoustics, some congregations try to alleviate the situation with drapes or ceiling tiles, which are often inconsistent with the original construction.

Today many facilities are fully integrating many of the above features. Although most all groups plan on additions in the future, many today start with a facility that will fulfill their primary needs for the present and near term but also can be added onto in the future. Many modern day facilities have the form and function capable of multifaceted support.

Chapter Three
THE MARKET FOR RELIGIOUS FACILITIES

*B*ecause the value of many facilities is a function of how many potential users/buyers there are in a given area, it will be important for the appraiser who values a religious facility to have some general knowledge about the presence or existence of various religious groups (buyers/sellers) in the area. Given the function of a typical religious facility, the relationship between the facilities and the users is paramount to the valuation process.

In general religious facilities tend to operate on a local basis. Other than a mega facility, most religious facilities function in and draw members from a very localized market. As a particular neighborhood evolves, the likely users of a given facility generally will be consistent with the neighborhood. Individuals typically practice their religion near their home and with individuals whose beliefs, socioeconomic standards, and values are similar. Thus, trends in an area tend to influence the valuation of a particular facility.

As the diversity of religious groups has grown, so has the need for religious facilities. Historically religious groups in the United States have been somewhat geographically segmented. This is becoming less so over time but still persists to a degree.

A chapter in the book *One Nation Under God—Religion in Contemporary American Society*[1] deals with the influence of geography on religious groups in the United States. This chapter, titled "Geography Is Destiny," implies that, in a certain way, the religious beliefs likely to influence a person will depend on where that person lives. The general conclusion of this chapter indicates that four basic groups tend to exist geographically as follows: Baptists in the South, Lutherans in the upper Midwest farm belt, Roman Catholics in the Northeast, and Mormons in Utah and the other Rocky Mountain states. This tends to be a rather macro view of religious groups, yet in general, may provide appraisers with a view of the areas in which they might be appraising. Although these are generalities, demand for religious facilities fulfilling individual needs tends to parallel this general summary. Other interesting findings relate to the diversity occurring in the newly expanding mega-cities of Southern California and Texas. The existence of immigrants and differing cultures in many markets throughout the country is expanding

---

1 Barry A. Kosmin and Seymour P. Lachman, *One Nation Under God: Religion in Contemporary American Society* (New York: Crown Publishers, Inc., 1993).

ethnic houses of worship.

Growth areas of the country are becoming very diverse, following the population trends in those areas. Ethnic patterns among religious groups are evidenced by such examples as the Korean Presbyterian Church, the Asian Christian Church, and the Chinese Christian Church among others. Additionally, the desire for schools, day care, and other similar services has caused individuals to mix their religious needs with their community needs. Obviously, religious or ethnic factors *do not* influence value, but the existence of users does influence the demand side of the equation and, therefore, value. As indicated in Advisory Opinion 16, "If the appraiser can identify the market behavior of the religious members and relate that behavior to the assignment, the appraiser is not in violation of USPAP."

In total, the need for facilities has paralleled areas of growth and ethnic diversity. Stable areas such as New England have had a nominal demand for new and/or existing facilities, whereas growth corridors in Florida, California, and Texas have been meccas for new facilities. These factors tend to provide a general framework for the appraiser to determine the likely demand for a new or existing facility in particular markets. As with most real estate, aberrations exist.

A recent survey of the various denominations that exist throughout the United States is summarized in *One Nation Under God—Religion in Contemporary American Society.* The random survey of 113,000 people from across the country was conducted by the Graduate School of the City University of New York by means of computer-generated telephone calls over a 13-month period. This National Survey of Religious Identifications is reportedly the largest and most comprehensive survey on the subject ever taken and includes not only the religious composition of the country but the geographic diversification. The question generally asked in the survey was: "What is your religion?" The results of the survey are summarized as follows:

Christian	86.2%
None	8.2%
Other Religions	3.3%
Refused	2.3%

In this survey the "None" category consisted of "agnostic," "humanist," and simply "no religion." The "Other Religions" category consisted of Jewish (the largest component of this category), Muslim/Islamic, Unitarian Universalist, Buddhist, Hindu, Native American, Scientologist, Baha'i, Taoist, New Age, Eckankar, Rastafarian, Sikh, Wiccan, Shintoist, Deity, and "other unclassified."

Interesting from a valuation standpoint was the geographic diversity of this group. The survey would indicate to the appraiser that almost 90% of the population of the United States is aligned with a religious group. Thus, the need for facilities appears apparent. The survey recognizes that not all of the respondents participate in organized religion, but given these numbers, many individuals do practice organized religion, indicating the need/demand for facilities.

The above noted survey is of individuals and not facilities. Conversations with a firm[2] specializing in tallying the religious facilities in the country has provided a detailed breakdown of the number and general denomination of religious facilities throughout the country. This information tends to indicate that there are approximately 345,000 facilities in the country. A breakdown of these facilities by religious denomination appears in the following tables.

These tables tend to indicate where facilities currently exist and, therefore, where demand for facilities will likely continue to exist. Nonetheless, this does not account for the microeconomics that tends to influence real estate demand and values. Additionally, these data do not account for areas of the country that are growing or in need of additional facilities.

Obviously, typical real estate needs are very localized, and thus the appraiser would need to look very carefully at the composition of the locale of the existing or proposed facility. The local telephone directory is an excellent source of information on area denominations as well as potential needs or buyers. Growing religious groups tend to sway what occurs in a particular area, which growth can be a function of a particular leader or facility.

It is important to understand what is typical for an area in terms of religious facilities. This will provide the appraiser with a foundation for understanding if a particular religious facility that is being valued fits the norm for the needs of predominant religious groups in the area. In other words, a large Baptist church in the South will have a larger universe of potential buyers than it would if it were located in New England since there are more Baptist churches in the South than in New England. This concept is significant to the valuation process of religious facilities. It should be noted, however, that the general religious trends noted here must be tempered with what is occurring in the local market, as is the case with most real estate.

This chapter has attempted to provide an overview of religious groups and therefore religious facilities throughout the country. Although the composition of the religious groups has little, if any, influence on value, the numbers of each and their growth factors do tend to identify potential users/buyers. It is important to emphasize that typical religious facilities exist on a local level, both from a use and a potential sale standpoint. Thus, it is imperative that the local characteristics that influence a facility be analyzed carefully. Many times this local level will be consistent with regional trends, but oftentimes aberrations will exist. Thus, as with most real estate, it is necessary to look carefully at both the macro and the micro market in which the facility is operating. A possible exception to this local market methodology involves larger facilities that might present a national market for a user.

---

2 American Church Lists, Inc., Arlington, Texas.

Number of Religious Facilities in the United States, by Denomination

State	Adventist	Baptist	Methodist	Lutheran	Presbyterian	Pentecostal	Catholic	Brethren	Independent Fundamentalist	Episcopal	Christian Churches of Christ	Mennonite	Mormon	Holiness	Metaphysical	Orthodox	Evangelical, Misc.	Misc./ Classified*	Totals
Alabama	70	4,682	1,701	103	474	1,400	151	7	46	130	1,151	7	36	289	38	7	281	72	10,645
Alaska	28	134	34	48	52	148	69	7	29	45	60	2	25	51	16	82	125	53	1,008
Arizona	65	684	133	235	182	621	209	16	79	70	305	18	212	173	112	21	316	150	3,611
Arkansas	80	3,058	755	91	271	1,160	111	1	39	59	1,059	10	37	171	35	6	214	37	7,194
California	580	3,591	895	1,029	1,264	4,358	1,268	114	382	473	1,442	101	374	1,016	1,128	219	2,605	1,473	22,312
Colorado	83	627	277	287	299	528	265	15	99	101	325	38	98	208	109	21	420	172	3,972
Connecticut	47	319	182	130	347	350	437	2	29	198	78	11	55	81	59	185	171	—	2,681
Washington, DC	17	283	69	17	32	158	50	4	9	41	31	5	1	32	43	13	80	44	930
Delaware	12	99	183	21	52	113	44	4	8	42	26	7	4	50	11	4	55	19	754
Florida	218	3,393	994	436	654	2,249	456	52	113	324	901	44	76	570	287	101	855	407	12,130
Georgia	120	4,991	1,626	136	493	1,585	144	2	39	164	762	9	44	334	78	19	390	144	11,080
Hawaii	29	98	34	25	91	165	78	4	13	43	65	2	36	57	38	3	115	222	1,117
Idaho	58	186	85	94	89	196	89	10	47	42	110	9	305	109	31	4	128	31	1,623
Illinois	189	3,351	1,738	1,281	1,252	2,040	1,202	81	287	215	1,271	86	135	767	240	106	1,104	521	15,866
Indiana	115	1,792	1,356	480	558	1,201	465	242	111	87	1,378	119	53	1,027	109	45	768	144	10,050
Iowa	82	568	1,122	949	789	427	558	62	102	73	457	40	110	224	55	15	376	98	6,107
Kansas	76	924	855	344	374	564	392	59	89	86	682	139	76	344	51	13	338	57	5,463
Kentucky	55	3,381	943	75	444	911	300	15	37	81	1,513	32	22	389	31	4	290	57	8,580
Louisiana	58	3,111	672	102	202	1,039	555	2	47	93	393	3	29	148	46	9	267	118	6,894
Maine	54	361	177	25	242	160	159	4	25	79	48	3	19	83	74	7	114	30	1,464
Maryland	102	827	1,009	328	300	677	278	100	85	248	176	46	26	189	87	23	375	177	5,053
Massachusetts	76	555	285	106	550	322	809	1	27	263	77	2	15	118	272	96	296	259	4,108
Michigan	233	2,128	1,098	1,010	1,047	1,442	863	102	279	260	491	81	171	848	224	83	784	301	11,445
Minnesota	67	443	283	2,001	379	330	519	5	57	103	151	25	36	180	82	24	496	106	5,291
Mississippi	63	3,394	1,085	49	344	863	135	18	83	539	11	27	122	20	5	146	61	—	6,965
Missouri	151	3,296	1,077	441	613	1,447	518	29	79	106	1,528	45	221	429	97	25	515	141	10,758
Montana	50	201	165	261	122	163	159	3	37	49	125	17	84	121	30	5	151	41	1,784
Nebraska	70	273	496	667	354	254	342	11	70	72	249	29	40	144	30	15	205	65	3,386
Nevada	17	128	31	36	24	122	57	15	32	53	73	27	28	8	75	35	—	—	761
New Hampshire	39	195	113	23	184	68	143	1	26	53	32	9	23	49	15	81	35	—	1,089
New Jersey	80	903	734	304	706	602	772	9	141	301	129	10	20	178	104	113	446	408	5,960
New Mexico	55	506	163	68	120	400	206	7	23	50	279	4	58	77	42	8	163	65	2,294
New York	259	1,927	1,665	718	1,510	1,761	1,858	11	148	748	400	53	67	673	324	231	965	1,484	14,801
North Carolina	156	5,956	2,462	325	1,163	2,193	160	20	44	270	797	18	56	523	75	13	801	152	15,184
North Dakota	52	119	169	739	180	120	257	6	10	29	24	17	18	69	10	7	88	22	1,936

[continued]

Number of Religious Facilities in Largest Metropolitan Areas of U.S.

State	Adventist	Baptist	Methodist	Lutheran	Presbyterian	Pentecostal	Catholic	Bretheran	Independent Funda-mentalist	Episcopal	Christian Churches of Christ	Mennonite	Mormon	Holiness	Metaphysical	Orthodox	Evangelical, Misc.	Misc./ Classified*	Totals
Ohio	17	2,804	2,183	924	1,236	2,027	1,023	351	143	213	1,395	166	94	1,226	243	147	1,112	373	15,887
Oklahoma	123	2,802	722	142	267	1,474	205	8	59	67	1,250	61	87	410	66	10	425	82	8,278
Oregon	139	486	216	241	210	626	182	12	68	102	397	41	119	263	116	11	434	146	3,829
Pennsylvania	231	1,755	2,780	1,636	2,156	1,281	1,682	412	345	432	481	466	1,045	1,045	161	283	1,027	470	16,696
Rhode Island	11	107	32	18	41	52	144	7	63	10	5	10	21	10	37	30	—	—	598
South Carolina	61	2,901	1,185	199	566	1,132	100	4	40	170	240	4	31	246	33	10	223	78	7,223
South Dakota	33	167	196	525	274	119	247	6	16	90	63	35	24	110	12	2	88	28	2,035
Tennessee	132	4,414	1,614	125	817	1,395	127	20	40	126	1,904	7	320	320	49	10	404	102	11,64+
Texas	268	8,476	2,424	894	888	4,008	1,197	38	230	456	3,359	47	573	573	264	49	1,342	308	25,038
Utah	18	113	22	32	39	74	85	14	22	33	511	13	5	5	39	31	—	—	1,071
Vermont	22	96	103	13	187	36	116	4	14	53	30	7	32	32	36	5	90	24	873
Virginia	109	2,955	1,779	292	762	1,190	200	217	64	375	689	72	303	303	86	26	393	142	9,696
Washington	166	712	276	495	403	781	283	32	130	149	340	12	351	351	167	16	625	199	5,256
Wisconsin	99	534	605	1,743	535	503	943	5	98	133	180	24	181	181	109	34	414	145	6,521
West Virginia	92	1,178	1,317	68	278	717	135	66	45	92	533	15	314	314	19	20	202	49	5,155
Wyoming	50	158	45	77	49	119	55	4	19	54	66	60	14	14	7	53	20	—	888

City	Adventist	Baptist	Methodist	Lutheran	Presbyterian	Pentecostal	Catholic	Bretheran	Independent Funda-mentalist	Episcopal	Christian Churches of Christ	Mennonite	Mormon	Holiness	Metaphysical	Orthodox	Evangelical, Misc.	Misc./ Classified*	Totals
Atlanta	39	1,694	511	81	216	462	55	1	20	56	271	7	10	97	46	10	147	72	3,795
Boston	13	146	56	23	88	98	180	0	7	68	11	3	4	30	73	27	60	93	980
Chicago	35	893	153	197	157	570	304	5	55	38	80	10	8	98	7+	35	284	185	3,181
Dallas	22	1,038	265	84	124	505	59	0	67	62	319	8	16	62	40	8	161	33	2,873
Denver	41	322	108	175	191	268	126	7	50	56	132	8	33	92	61	13	246	99	2,037
Fort Worth	33	768	172	46	72	329	45	2	33	34	251	1	11	49	21	3	114	17	2,001
Houston	31	1,347	315	173	134	724	209	8	39	87	381	2	57	84	59	17	239	76	3,962
Los Angeles	105	953	205	215	358	922	301	36	76	88	303	9	89	214	298	52	564	445	5,213
New York	135	643	223	231	307	870	532	6	48	191	162	16	8	149	115	107	371	976	5,090
Phoenix	27	400	88	131	106	375	104	6	41	36	135	15	110	95	66	15	176	82	2,003
Salt Lake City	8	80	17	23	32	53	55	0	10	14	24	0	364	9	16	4	32	35	766
San Francisco	69	674	136	156	182	568	229	4	47	90	141	6	35	122	171	46	317	260	3,253

* This category includes facilities for the following religions: Baha'i, Buddhist, Zen, Eckankar, Hindu, Jehovah's Witnesses, Jewish, Krishna, Muslim/Islamic, Sikh, Spiritualist Church/Organizations, Tenikyo Churches, Unification Church, Unitarian Universalist Association, United Synagogue of America, Yoga Institute, and miscellaneous cults and sects.

Source: American Church Lists, Inc., Arlington, Texas

Chapter Four
THE PHYSICAL FACILITY

The purpose of this section is not to provide a complete architectural analysis or dissertation on religious facilities themselves, but to acquaint the reader sufficiently with major physical elements or characteristics that may be observed when inspecting and valuing a facility. As with most appraisal problems, being a generalist can be particularly insightful in the valuation process. There are many facets to religious facilities that require differing skills to recognize and value. This chapter should acquaint the reader with the various types and particular features of religious facilities.

Because many religious facilities fulfill more than just a worship service function, peripheral areas and activities are expanding. Many of the following features may be found in religious facilities today. In some properties only a few of these items will be present but in others, many will be found.

- Sanctuary
- Chapel
- Narthex (entry area)
- Baptistery
- Mikva (ritual bath)
- Bell tower
- Meeting rooms
- Administrative offices
- Choir room
- Quiet room
- Cry rooms (room for small children with access and visibility to the sanctuary)
- Library
- Classrooms
- Kitchen
- Gym

- Theater
- Concert hall
- Community center
- Media room and/or broadcast studio
- Bookstore
- Restaurant
- Day care center
- Nursing home
- Family life center
- Outreach facilities
- Field activities
- Parking garage
- Amusement park
- Game room
- Dance hall
- Rectory
- Parsonage

The design of some religious facilities is congregation-specific and consistent with the members' needs and desires. A facility with a unique or "contemporary" design is often more expensive to build than a more conventionally designed facility of similar ceiling height, quality of materials, seating, etc. From a marketability standpoint, as long as the facility is functional, typically there is no measurable value difference between such a facility and a more conventional facility.

The expansion of religious facilities has been a function of need. While some of the features listed here fulfill the needs of the religious group itself, others such as gyms, game rooms, and concert or dance hall may be oriented to and necessitated by the community in which the religious body functions. Although small neighborhood religious facilities are probably the norm, the mega-facility containing all of the above is becoming more common. Many people want to belong to a religious facility (physical facility) that parallels their own lifestyles. Thus, very expensive and elaborate facilities tend to be built in areas where the inhabitants can afford to support the facilities. As with most real estate, however, aberrations exist. Some congregations in relatively middle-income areas or with middle-income congregants have built some excellent quality facilities and manage to collect significant sums from their members. Conversely, smaller and less ornate facilities are being built in moderately affluent areas. Some religious groups take pride in "simple" or "small" facilities for any number of reasons.

Newer facilities may be traditional or contemporary in design and appearance depending in part on the congregation's wants and needs. Typical of a modern religious facility is the classic red brick structure with columns or pillars defining the central entrance, and with a large sanctuary and wings on one or both sides for classrooms and/or

The bell tower in this contemporary facility is nonfunctional and was built for visual appeal only. The exterior of the building is stucco. The facility is part of a campus of older, more traditional buildings. The rear of this building is visible from a street that provides the main entrance to a small city. As such, residents in the area are readily aware of the facility's presence. This photograph shows the entrance to the sanctuary.

administrative functions. On the other hand, it is also common today for the design to be contemporary with a stucco exterior and an unusual shape.

Most religious facilities evolve over time. It is not uncommon to find religious facilities with several older buildings that previously fulfilled other needs. Although consistent in exterior appearance, the facility represents an evolution of the religious group itself. A well-planned facility lends itself well to this type of expansion. Today's campus-like facilities have evolved in this manner.

The quality of construction varies significantly in religious facilities. Some may have been built with donated labor or material, which may or may not meet local building codes or quality standards. The appraiser must be careful to analyze the true quality of construction of the facility. Some facilities are built over an extended period—sometimes years—as funds are available. This factor becomes relevant in the estimate of depreciation and cost new. It also affects the consistency of the ultimate finish of the facility. Thus, a facility could be functionally adequate, yet the overall finish could be inferior by typical or local standards.

In general, religious facilities will tend to follow the group's needs, desires, and perceptions of themselves. In the resale market, some groups may be willing to compromise these needs, desires, and perceptions to obtain an older facility that may not fully serve them but may appear as a bargain relative to the alternative of new construction.

Thus, congregations may be willing to compromise their desires and needs to purchase a facility at less than the depreciated cost.

The following will acquaint the reader with the various types of facilities, improvements, and other specialty items incidental to religious facilities.

STYLES OF RELIGIOUS FACILITIES

Older "Classic" Facilities

Numerous books have been written on the architecture of the older, ornate religious facilities of the 1800s and early 1900s. Many of these facilities are located in downtown districts or urban areas. Most have insufficient parking by modern standards. Typically they consist of a large sanctuary with some peripheral classrooms or administrative offices. Many have high ceilings, extensive stained glass, hardwood pews, and unusual roof designs and whose construction is inconsistent with modern standards. Examples include facilities in medieval gothic, Romanesque or Greek design and style. Such intricate designs would be very difficult to reproduce today. Many larger and newer facilities are built around the original and smaller facilities.

Modern Facilities

Many facilities built today frequently tend to use a traditional design with a (red) brick facade, a high ceiling/roof, pillars, and possibly a pitched roof line. Alternatively, numerous newly built facilities can be found which are very functional in design; they may have unusual shapes and harsh lines, use "modern" colors, and have a stucco exterior. There does not appear to be a consistent trend in the preference for a contemporary look versus the more classic design. Facilities are generally consistent with the desires and beliefs of the group proposing the facility. Religious groups that profess to live the simple life tend to gravitate to more traditional architecture. Others that are progressive or consider themselves modern tend toward a more "contemporary" look.

The Evolving Facility

A recent development in the evolution of religious facilities is the "family life center," which stems from the expanding role that some congregations play in their members' lives. This typically is a building developed as "flex space" to provide a forum for the multitude of needs occurring in an expanding congregation. These facilities can often double as sanctuaries, dining areas, meeting halls, education centers, administrative areas, and gyms.

Another recent trend involves the conversion of retail space. While the use of store fronts by religious groups, particularly as start-up operations, has a long history in some urban areas, this concept has been expanded in some parts of the country by the conversion of larger retail facilities into houses of worship. This phenomenon has been spurred by the economic downturn in various communities during the 1980s and early 1990s. Many neighborhood retail centers failed when the anchor either left or failed, or the needs of the

The Appraisal of Religious Facilities

The issue of highest and best use becomes critical in the valuation of "converted" religious facilities—i.e., properties originally built for another purpose (e.g., an industrial building [top] or retail center [bottom]). While these properties may become available for religious purposes during periods of economic downturn, if the economy recovers, the current use must be examined in light of alternative uses that are feasible and maximally profitable.

community could not support the center. The advent of the big box retailer also put an end to many neighborhood centers. As these centers became available for any number of reasons, religious groups identified them as practically ideal for a religious facility. Typically, the anchor space is converted into the sanctuary, and the balance of the local retail space is converted into classrooms and administrative space. As retail centers need significant parking, this situation is typically available. An aspect that hinders this type of development is that no matter how hard the congregation or architect tries, the facilities still "look" like retail centers. Thus, although functional, the design and appeal is not as desirable as a facility built as a religious facility.

As with many "converted" facilities, the issue of highest and best use is a critical element in the valuation/appraisal process. Typically, when a retail center, warehouse, or other facility becomes available during periods of economic downturn, the "ultimate" highest and best use is always a question. Over time if the economy recovers, a facility's highest and best use can obviously change. This factor is paramount to the valuation of the site and the facility in total if an alternative use would be feasible and maximally profitable.

TYPICAL FEATURES

Sanctuary

The sanctuary, or worship space, is the focal point of most religious structures. Often this space is the most expensive to build and provides the building with much of its value. For the most part, sanctuaries do not differ significantly among the majority of users, although certain religious groups may have unique requirements. For example, in synagogues or temples in Reform Judaism, the ark, which contains the Torah(s), is generally placed against the wall that faces Jerusalem. Thus, the congregation faces Jerusalem. Some orthodox synagogues have divided seating with men on one side and women on the other.

A sanctuary is generally designed to seat a large majority of the members of the group at one time and directs attention to one or more altar areas, pulpits, and/or lecterns. In synagogues, the reader's platform is called a bema (or bemah). Other features of a sanctuary may include an organ loft, choir stalls, a baptistery or baptismal pool or font, an ark (i.e., Torah area), and one or more balconies. Numerous aesthetically pleasing elements may be added such as high-beamed ceilings, stained glass, paintings, carvings, and statuary as well as extensive overhead and specialty lighting, drapes, and other items. Such elements are incorporated to make the space special and dramatic and also to foster a sense of worship. As the central locus of the facility, the sanctuary must be consistent with the focus of the organization and its beliefs.

Sanctuaries are designed in various configurations but generally they have much in common as can be seen in the accompanying floor plans.

Typically the sanctuary area is designed for an audience or congregation to hear one or more speakers and also, perhaps, to hear a variety of vocal and/or instrumental music (either live or recorded). To improve the congregants' view of the events or speakers, it is

Rectilinear Sanctuary (Small)
First Floor Plan

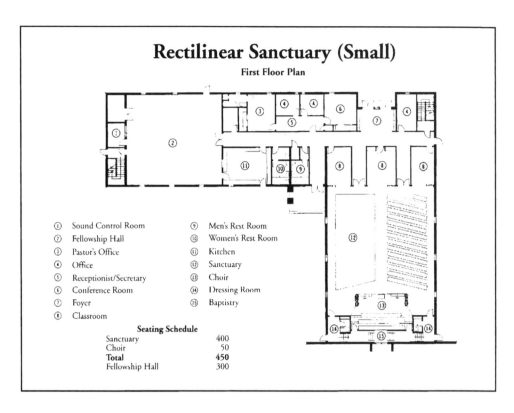

①	Sound Control Room	⑨	Men's Rest Room
②	Fellowship Hall	⑩	Women's Rest Room
③	Pastor's Office	⑪	Kitchen
④	Office	⑫	Sanctuary
⑤	Receptionist/Secretary	⑬	Choir
⑥	Conference Room	⑭	Dressing Room
⑦	Foyer	⑮	Baptistry
⑧	Classroom		

Seating Schedule

Sanctuary	400
Choir	50
Total	**450**
Fellowship Hall	300

Fan Sanctuary (Small)
First Floor Plan

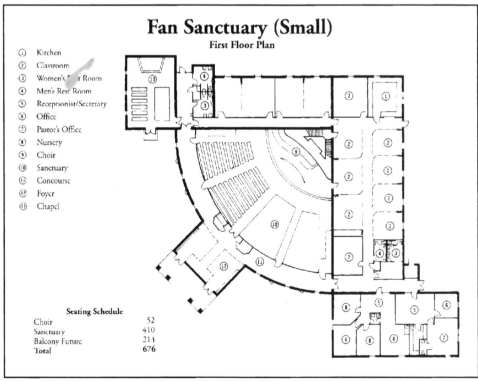

①	Kitchen
②	Classroom
③	Women's Rest Room
④	Men's Rest Room
⑤	Receptionist/Secretary
⑥	Office
⑦	Pastor's Office
⑧	Nursery
⑨	Choir
⑩	Sanctuary
⑪	Concourse
⑫	Foyer
⑬	Chapel

Seating Schedule

Choir	52
Sanctuary	410
Balcony Future	214
Total	**676**

Source: Roe Messner, *Building for the Master: By Design* (Wichita, Kansas: RAM Media, Inc., 1987).

Square Sanctuary (Medium)

① Fellowship Hall
② Foyer
③ Kitchen
④ Fireside Room
⑤ Men's Rest Room
⑥ Women's Rest Room
⑦ Nursery
⑧ Receptionist/Secretary
⑨ Office
⑩ Library
⑪ Pastor's Office
⑫ Classroom
⑬ Prayer Room
⑭ Choir Practice Room
⑮ Sanctuary
⑯ Choir
⑰ Baptistry

Seating Schedule

Sanctuary	1000
Choir	60
Total	**1060**

Square Sanctuary (Large)
First Floor Plan

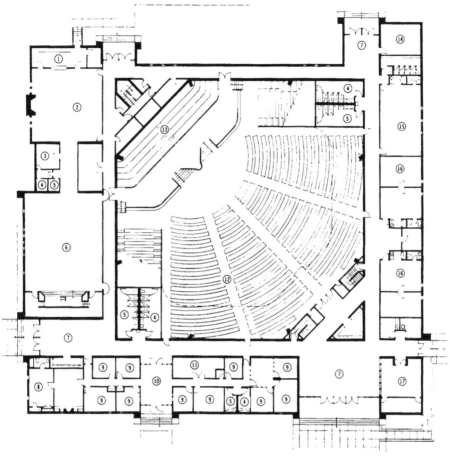

①	Kitchen	⑩	Receptionist/Secretary
②	Parlor/Board Room	⑪	Work Room
③	Bride's Room	⑫	Sanctuary
④	Women's Rest Room	⑬	Choir
⑤	Men's Rest Room	⑭	Dressing Room
⑥	Chapel	⑮	Children's Choir Room
⑦	Foyer	⑯	Nursery
⑧	Pastor's Office	⑰	Bookstore
⑨	Office		

Seating Schedule

Sanctuary	780
Choir	120
Balcony	780
Total	**1680**

Octagon Sanctuary (Medium)

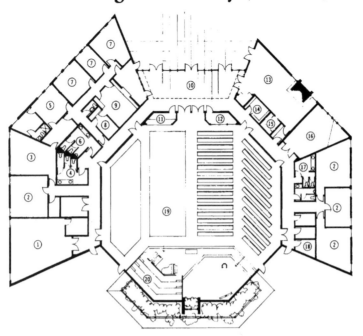

①	Choir Practice Room	⑪	Sound Control Room
②	Classroom	⑫	Cry Room
③	Conference Room	⑬	Fireside Room
④	Women's Rest Room	⑭	Library
⑤	Pastor's Office	⑮	Kitchen
⑥	Men's Rest Room	⑯	Chapel
⑦	Office	⑰	Women's Rest Room
⑧	Work Room	⑱	Sacristy
⑨	Receptionist/Secretary	⑲	Sanctuary
⑩	Narthex	⑳	Choir

Seating Schedule

Sanctuary	652
Choir	60
Total	**712**

Rectilinear Sanctuary (Large)
First Floor Plan

1. Choir Practice Room
2. Audio Control
3. Video Control
4. Orchestra Room
5. Classroom
6. Office
7. Work Room
8. Teacher's Lounge
9. Nurse's Room
10. Library
11. Kitchen
12. Choir
13. Orchestra
14. Sanctuary
15. Men's Rest Room
16. Women's Rest Room
17. Bookstore
18. Nursery
19. Foyer
20. Rear Projection Room
21. Ushers Room
22. Conference Room
23. Counseling Room
24. Pastor's Office
25. Receptionist/Secretary
26. Fellowship Hall

Seating Schedule

Sanctuary	2330
Choir	200
Total	**2530**

common for the sanctuary area to be designed with a clear span. With the advent of video and TV monitors, many facilities today broadcast the service into other areas of the facility, making the sanctuary less important. Nonetheless, without question, the sanctuary is typically the focal point of a religious facility.

Items to analyze in the sanctuary are its design, ceiling height, type of seating, view angles (unobstructed or not), acoustics, lighting, flooring, access/traffic patterns, and rest room access. The presence of such features as stained glass windows, artwork, a baptistery, one or more balconies, organ or choir loft, and sound systems, etc., should be noted. Some sanctuaries are built to accentuate a nearby view (via windows) or an item specific to the particular religion.

Religious facilities often refer to the entrance area/foyer or hallway outside of the sanctuary as the narthex. This area, which often serves as a gathering place or welcoming zone, should be adequate for the size of the sanctuary. The narthex may also provide access to rest rooms or other parts of the facility as well as to stairs and/or elevators. The area can be simple or elaborate.

In addition to the main sanctuary, one or more chapels may be present. They generally are built for more intimate occasions such as small weddings, christenings, etc., and thus are usually smaller than the sanctuary. They may, however, be relatively ornate in design, with fixed seating, a pulpit, stained or leaded glass and high ceilings. Many times a chapel is the original sanctuary of a facility which has grown over time and has built a larger sanctuary.

Sanctuary Seating

Paramount to most religious facilities is the need to seat the entire congregation, even if only several times each year. Many houses of worship have pews, or bench-like seats, in the sanctuary or chapel although in some cases theater-type seats are used. Most pews are made of hardwood or veneer. While some pews have no backs or padding, most are constructed with backs and some have seat and back padding. Some may also have book holders and kneelers depending on the religion. Pews and theater-type seats are generally affixed to the floor. Although technically removable, given the function and nature of this type of seating, it is reasonable to consider pews or theater seats a fixture and therefore part of the real estate. Pews are often a separately contracted item when facilities are built. It is prudent for the appraiser to inquire if they were included in the total cost when analyzing actual costs.

Some facilities use portable chairs, which may be connected together or simply freestanding. Typically, chairs are considered personal property as they are not affixed to the real estate. In some cases, however, they may be sufficiently sanctuary-specific in color, design, or method of affixing, etc., for them to be included as part of the real estate for valuation purposes.

Seating capacity is typically set by the local fire marshal or building/zoning ordinances. For an appraisal, actual seating available mandated by these sources is the relevant

The ceiling of this modern synagogue consists of eight pairs of poured-in-place concrete vaults; between each vault is a panel of amber-tinted glass, creating an "architecture of light." Central to the sanctuary is the ark, which rests on a white marble bema (or altar) and is sheltered by a rising form that symbolizes the traditional Jewish prayer shawl.

amount of seating that should be assumed for the facility. Many facilities quote seating that is best described as "maximum capacity." In confirming sales it is best to ask for the legally permissible maximum seating. This is an important benchmark in describing the subject and in the analysis of the comparables.

Because the sanctuary represents one of the costliest elements, the ratio of sanctuary space or seating to total area is an important issue. Older religious facilities are typically comprised primarily of sanctuary space and, as such, have a ratio of seating to total area that is relatively low (e.g., 10 to 30 square feet of total building area per seat or seating capacity. That is to say, each seat supports approximately 10 to 30 square feet of total building area.) As religious facilities have expanded their activities and become more involved in the day-to-day lives of their members, this ratio has increased as more peripheral area is needed. It is now not uncommon to find religious facilities with a ratio of seating to total square feet in excess of 60 square feet for each sanctuary seat. However, one may also find modern facilities with ratios in the range of 30 to 40 square feet of sanctuary space for each square foot of total area, with little or no noticeable influence on marketability. How the space is utilized and its flexibility are important to this issue.

As a cautionary note, these ratios must be monitored carefully. A low ratio of seating to total building area does not always indicate that a facility is not functional by modern standards. Some congregations (and parts of the country) need large sanctuaries to seat their entire membership once or twice per week while others that are primarily teaching facilities need more peripheral space. Local desires and needs must be analyzed.

Stained Glass

Some houses of worship, especially older ones, have ornate glass or decorative windows. Stained glass is typically a thin, colored glass held in place by lead strips. Many older stained glass windows are protected from the elements by a plastic or glass exterior window. Other decorative glass consists of art painted on glass. One process consists of a rubberized color coating over the glass. Painted glass typically is not very valuable and can be easily removed. More recently, there has been a propensity toward faceted glass windows, in which thick pieces of colored glass are held in place by mortar. Faceted glass windows typically depict a person, theme, or story relevant to the group occupying the facility. Some leaded/stained glass windows and faceted glass windows are very expensive and need to be carefully analyzed. The nature or type of window should be accurately identified. The removal of a large stained glass or faceted glass window can be prohibitively expensive, often approaching the replacement cost of the glass. Faceted glass and stained glass windows are generally valued separately on a per-square-foot basis. They are usually considered a fixture.

Organs

Many houses of worship will have one or more organs in their sanctuaries. Simpler electronic organs are typically personal property and should not be included in the value of the real estate appraised. When organs are sufficiently "attached" to the facility or are the focal point of a sanctuary, they could be construed as part of the structure or real estate. This is particularly the case with elaborate pipe organs, which are sufficiently attached to the building so as to make their removal unsightly or cause "serious injury to the real estate." Since such instruments can cost in excess of one million dollars, an organ expert may be hired to determine value, should this become an issue. Any market data developed should be carefully analyzed to determine how an organ was accounted for.

Sound Systems

Sound systems, if present, are typically considered a part of the sanctuary. Many sanctuaries are developed by professional sound engineers and have custom-made speakers, amplifiers, microphones, mixers, and other sound-related items. To the extent that the sound system operates in harmony with the room, it is best described as a fixture and should be valued as a part of the real estate.

In today's world of televangelists and television broadcasting, it is becoming more common for sanctuaries also to be fitted with monitors, broadcast equipment, and other peripheral recording capabilities. For the most part, these items are not typically fixtures. An exception is a monitor system for a nursery, "cry room" (a separate sound-proof room where infants can be attended to by parents or others during a service), or other areas of the sanctuary with poor sight lines. An argument for including sound systems as a fixture in the valuation is that the function of the sanctuary is to provide a forum or arena for worship, singing, or preaching, and without the sound system, this function is severely impaired.

Many religious facilities record services for further use or for a library, and some do live broadcasts. This recording equipment is not typically considered a fixture, even though it is built in and may function as part of the room in which it exists. If such equipment is included as real estate, it should be valued by an expert. In some instances the congregation owns a radio station/license, which includes broadcasting facilities, studios, antennas, and other peripheral items. In these cases it is suggested that the appraiser hire an outside consultant to analyze and value the assets.

Rest Rooms

The number of rest rooms required is generally a function of local plumbing codes. As occupancy loads vary between areas of buildings and areas of the country, it is difficult to provide a benchmark for rest rooms. As a general rule of thumb, it is recommended that at least one men's and one women's fixture be available for each 100 seats in the sanctuary. One of the biggest problems is determining the ratio of men's rest rooms to women's rest rooms. In general there should be one and a half to two times more fixtures in a women's rest room than in a men's rest room.

Choir Rooms

Many religious organizations incorporate vocal and/or instrumental music into their services. This frequently requires rehearsal rooms (often with risers, stepped platforms, or slanted flooring) for choirs or instrumentalists. This space may also incorporate a music library, dressing rooms, and closets or storage areas for gowns. Some religious facilities, however, simply have their choir practice in the sanctuary.

Classrooms

Because many religious facilities offer education programs, generally tied to the teaching of religious doctrine, the need for classroom space is evident. Space for classes from preschool to adult education may be present, and many religious facilities even operate certified private primary and secondary schools. In some instances full college campuses have been integrated into the facility.

Care must be taken to determine if the area to be utilized as a private school is in compliance with local codes. In addition, cafeterias, sport facilities, and other items (lockers, additional administrative offices, gyms, etc.) often exist. Typically, these types of facilities are subject to significant local codes and standards.

Library

As part of the educational process, many large religious facilities have a library, which may be equipped with exchange counters, book return facilities, and built-in desks, etc. Some libraries are more similar to a bookstore and might sell books and religious items. Shelving can be built-in or removable. If removable, the shelves are considered personal property.

Another recent addition to many religious facilities is a media room and/or media library, designed for housing, viewing, and/or storing media items. With the advent of the VCR, these types of rooms are becoming more common. Often this room is located in conjunction with a theater designed for viewing films, plays, or other theatrical events.

Kitchens

A kitchen is an integral part of a typical religious facility. It may range from space simply for a microwave to a complete, commercial-grade restaurant setup. Some facilities have a snack bar, restaurant, or cafeteria on the premises, which is often a center or gathering point of the facility. Some are "profit" centers and others are simply designed to serve the members.

To the extent that kitchen equipment is consistent with the needs and design of the facility (and a typical user) and/or is built in, it is reasonable to consider such equipment a fixture and therefore part of the real estate. It is paramount to the operation of the facility. These items should be carefully analyzed and valued as they relate to the whole of the facility being appraised.

Sports and Entertainment Facilities

As religious groups attempt to serve the changing needs of the congregation, other special facilities are being added to host activities such as midnight basketball, dances, and other outreach programs. Gyms and related workout facilities are becoming more common, particularly in conjunction with a family life center. These facilities often include a basketball court, bleachers, stage, pools, weight rooms, racquetball/handball courts, locker rooms, and shower areas. Large overhead folding door (dividers) and special floors may be present.

Some facilities are creating recreational/entertainment areas such as nightclubs or social halls with stages, dance floors, sound and video equipment, special lighting, and snack areas to attract and provide an outlet for young people. Some religious groups are even developing miniature golf courses, pools, driving ranges, bowling alleys, football/sports fields, baseball fields, etc.

Parking

Religious facilities desire to have sufficient parking to accommodate the largest likely seating, and most facilities would prefer to have an excess of parking for growth or special events. Parking is typically tied to the size of the sanctuary but may relate to other activities provided at the facility. Parking requirements vary from area to area depending on zoning issues, building codes, and how the congregants attend the facility. For example, if on the average 350 members attend a given service and each household consists of 2.4 persons, a minimum of 146 parking spaces would be required just for members. Additional spaces for visitors and employees would also be needed. Congregations are often aware of their membership demographics and can help in this calculation.

The Uniform Building Code requires one parking space for every four seats in a given sanctuary/chapel or lecture hall. A rule of thumb for the Southern Baptist Convention is a 1:3 ratio of parking to seating. Conversations with several architects active in the design of religious facilities indicated a ratio of 2.2–2.5 spaces per seat is necessary for a modern and active congregation. The architects queried indicated that ultimately the need for parking is tied to the type of congregants. Parking requirements vary extensively depending on the situation. For example, a facility whose members are primarily families that attend four to five per car will have significantly different requirements than a facility that attracts singles who come one per car. Many organizations have buses that bring in the congregants, which greatly lowers the necessary on-site parking. Other areas of dense population may have a higher degree of "walk in" traffic or congregants may depend on public transportation.

Typically a facility would like to have adequate parking for any given situation, yet this is not always the case. Shortages of parking spaces are often the rule for religious facilities. It is not uncommon for congregations to solve their parking situation in a variety of ways. This can include on-street parking or using or renting vacant space in nearby school, office, or retail parking areas. Because peak parking for the religious facility may occur during off times for typical commercial establishments, this situation is often easily solvable. If sufficient parking is not available or easy to locate, this situation must be considered as it impacts the marketability and value of the subject. This can be a restriction to growth, in particular in CBD/downtown areas and other areas where little room for expansion exists.

For existing facilities the following question should be asked: Does the existing parking situation adequately fulfill the needs of the congregation (or a potential congregation) at periods of maximum use (assuming the facility is fully utilized) and is it consistent with the local zoning/building ordinance? The parking situation must be analyzed carefully relative to all of the above issues for both the subject and the comparables.

Conclusion

As with any type of property appraisal, the quality of a facility must be carefully analyzed, including the framing, fixtures, and type of finish as well as the complexity and quality of construction. Religious facilities can range from highly ornate stone and masonry structures to converted retail centers and metal buildings. As such, it is imperative to carefully analyze the subject relative to the comparables (cost comparables and sales comparables) in order to account for quality. In particular, when using cost comparables, it is important to determine if the costs provided include donated materials or labor.

The preceding discussion attempts to delineate most religious facility attributes that may be encountered by the appraiser. As is evidenced from the above discussions, many religious facilities are expanding physically to fulfill members' needs and are likely continue doing so in the future.

Chapter Five
LAND VALUE

The highest and best use of a site is paramount to the foundation of valuation. The valuation of the site or land for a religious facility starts with the premise that the facility is fulfilling a need in the community. This is no different than it would be for a retail center, day care facility, or other neighborhood support facility. A difference does exist, however, that due to the nonprofit nature of religious facilities, it is practically impossible to apply the test of financial feasibility in a highest and best use analysis. Nonetheless, religious groups often compete with retail or residential development or other market participants to purchase sites for their facilities. Thus, subject to zoning requirements and any other restrictions, site values for religious facilities typically are consistent with other similarly zoned and/or located parcels of land.

Appraisers tend to research a community for sales of sites to religious facilities or other similar users. Although highly suggested, this methodology can be misleading because religious groups typically have to pay a price for their site(s) that is similar to *surrounding* land values. That is to say, religious facilities compete with *area-specific* users for sites with similar zoning, utility, restrictions, and highest and best uses. Thus, using the sale of a site to a religious facility or group from an area where values are more or less than the subject area's values can lead to erroneous value indications. Nonetheless, it is highly suggested to first analyze the area market for sales of sites to religious facilities or other nonprofit groups. This can provide evidence of the need for new neighborhood support facilities. If land use restrictions and zoning are similar, such sales can also support the value of the subject.

Because religious facilities can be constructed in many different zoning classifications, it is important to recognize that such groups may be competing with developer/buyers who have different specific projects or highest and best uses in mind. Other than very large congregations that draw from a regional area, religious facilities typically select sites in proximity to their members and are often competing with alternative users. Thus, in valuing a religious facility site, it is important to utilize areas in proximity to the subject or areas with similar needs and influences (income levels, interests, daily needs, etc.).

In rural or other areas with no zoning or use restrictions, the value of land for a religious facility tends to parallel that of sites most similar to it, i.e., competing sites with similar physical characteristics.

In cases of older religious facilities located in fully built-up areas, a land residual technique can be particularly helpful in estimating the value of residential or commercial land. This technique has many pitfalls, yet it provides one of the few alternatives in situations where no land sales have occurred for many years or where the area is 100% built out. Proper and reasonable application of the land residual technique is important in developing a reliable value estimate of the site as if vacant in fully developed areas.

Because most religious facilities assume they will grow over time, they have a propensity to acquire land in excess of their current needs. This is similar to the industrial property owner who has a large site next to his facility available for expansion. This "excess land" may not be truly excess in terms of value relative to the value of the developed portions of the site. Because growth is an integral goal of most religious groups, they tend to value the "excess site" area at the same level as the primary site. Therefore, unless the ratio of building area to site is excessive or the site can be readily "split off," it is suggested the site be valued in total in the final value estimate. Many lenders question this assumption, but typically a religious group will have plans for expansion, and thus the "excess land" is simply good planning for its perceived future. Excessively large sites relative to the facility (e.g., a 4,000-sq.-ft. facility on 30 acres) may actually have an alternative highest and best use. The same may be true of larger facilities on small sites.

As in valuing any site, the appraiser must take note of any adverse influences. For the site of a religious facility, these influences can be different from those for residential/commercial sites. Religious facilities need parking when many typical users do not (Saturday or Sunday mornings). Sites where loud noises exist (e.g., next to airports or rail lines) are probably inappropriate for religious facility use. Sites with a view or other aesthetic qualities are often desired by religious groups to add ambience to the facility. Other adverse influences could include:

- Poor access to a busy arterial

- Heavy industry

- Pollution

- Inconsistent land uses

- Flood hazard areas

- Lack of residences in area

- Areas of population decline

- Areas with use/legal restrictions against religious facility uses (houses of worship, day care, schools, etc.)

Positive attributes of sites for religious facility use include:

- Useable area plus room for expansion

- Proximity to traffic patterns (easy entry and exit or light-controlled access to nominally busy streets)

- Recognizable address (easy to find)

- Topography that allows easy construction

- Aesthetically pleasing environment (view, trees, pond, lake)

Obviously all other site attributes typically desired for the construction of improvements (soils, utilities, no flood plain influence, etc.) are considered positive attributes. Religious facilities are often granted items that a typical developer would not receive such as access to utilities and relaxed setback requirements that may make a particular site more "valuable." Conversely, due to traffic and parking issues associated with religious facilities, many communities are not open to new religious facility construction. For example, if a school is planned as part of the facility, permits for schools may be difficult to obtain in many areas of the country.

In conclusion, estimating the value of an existing site for a religious facility focuses first on the site's highest and best use. Once the highest and best use is determined, the typical valuation techniques are applied. Religious facilities have a place in the neighborhood equally as important and as valuable as other support facilities (commercial, retail, day care, etc.). The valuation of religious facilities needs to be carried out using acceptable methodology and techniques, and values should parallel those of similar area sites.

Chapter Six
THE COST APPROACH

The cost approach historically has been a principal valuation technique for special-use/single-purpose properties. Subject to its "proper and reasonable" application, this methodology appears appropriate for valuing religious facilities since they are by definition special-purpose properties and infrequently sold, and their value is often dictated in part by their cost, function, and design. Very specific analyses of cost new, depreciation, and land values are paramount to applying the cost approach properly. It is imperative that assumptions are based on actual and market-supported costs as much as possible. That is to say, with respect to special-use properties the valuation process starts with cost new. If this is not developed properly, the entire valuation process can be flawed.

The issue of reproduction cost new versus replacement cost is paramount to a discussion of the cost approach for single-purpose, special-use properties. Reproduction cost new implies constructing an exact duplicate of the existing improvements at today's costs. Replacement cost is the estimated cost to construct, at current prices, a building with equivalent utility.

In newer religious facilities reproduction cost and replacement cost are often the same or very similar. The issue, however, becomes acute in significantly older facilities built with obsolete or excessive building standards or with unusual materials, where reproducing the facility would be very different from replacing it. Consider, for example, an older urban house of worship with a very ornate design, high ceilings, overly thick walls, and an expensive, unusual copper roof. Developing reproduction costs for such a facility becomes difficult since building standards have changed and the labor and/or materials are simply not available to reproduce a particular facility or item. Regardless, reproduction cost new typically represents the cost basis for measuring depreciation from all causes. Most insurance companies prefer to provide replacement cost rather than reproduction cost coverage for older ornate facilities.

The use of replacement cost as the basis of cost new can eliminate the need to estimate some forms of functional obsolescence although other forms may still be present along with physical depreciation and external obsolescence. In measuring functional obsolescence using replacement cost estimates, it is still necessary to consider the additional costs of removing items of curable functional obsolescence (i.e., the cost to cure is less than the added contributory value). Any excess operating cost(s) associated with superadequate construction must also be considered. Replacement cost should eliminate the need to measure accrued depreciation due to excessive or superadequate construction. Care, however, must be taken in determining "superadequate construction" in a facility whose purpose is to inspire and provide a house of worship. Some congregations seek a simple house of worship, others seek palaces. What appears to be superadequate construction may simply be typical for that particular type of facility or religious group. A large facility without an ornate sanctuary (high ceilings, stained glass, etc.) could be considered inadequate. In newer and more modern facilities where no functional obsolescence is present, replacement cost often is very similar to reproduction cost.

The purpose of the appraisal can further complicate the use of replacement cost versus reproduction cost. An appraisal for insurance purposes might specifically request reproduction or replacement cost. Regardless of which is used, care must be taken to measure appropriately the depreciation that is influencing the property.

In the cost approach, the appraiser must first carefully inspect the subject property, which will serve as the basis for developing a cost new estimate. There are several sources of cost new along with numerous methods to test the reasonableness of the concluded costs. Since the total valuation model is extremely sensitive to the subject's cost new estimate, this process should be undertaken carefully.

SOURCES FOR COST NEW

One of the best indications of the total cost or cost new of a facility is actual cost. Assuming that the construction is relatively recent and that the facility was built in a workman-like manner and without a significant amount of donated labor or materials, actual cost is likely the best check for cost new.

Cost comparables based on information from builders, architects, city permit departments, bidding publications, and public announcements are a second category of support for the cost new estimate. Such data are often a mixed bag and must be sifted through for the relevant figures. It is imperative to determine if items such as land, indirect costs, site improvements, specialty items, etc., are specifically included before using the data. Typically these figures are total costs, and include site improvements, indirect costs, and specialty items, which makes these data an excellent check of cost new. When enough data are collected, frequently the information is very consistent with actual costs and cost service information.

National cost services such as Marshall & Swift are a third source of cost new data. Careful consideration must be made as to ceiling heights, percent of sanctuary space to total space, classroom or school space, unusual perimeters, enclosures, and other areas as well as the inclusion/exclusion of specialty items. Pews, organs, steeples, kitchen equipment, stained glass, pulpits, and sound systems are not normally included and should be accounted for if appropriate.

It is often necessary to identify various components of the facility separately due to vast differences in quality, design, intended use, and cost. Some facilities contain offices or office buildings, schools, day-care or independent living facilities, and other property types. To account for all of them, it may be more appropriate to estimate costs separately. There are numerous pitfalls to this methodology and it must be used with care. Most typically it is applied on a per-square-foot basis. Specialty items, however, must be added separately, typically on a lump-sum basis.

It may be necessary from time to time to refer to the segregated method of developing cost new. This is difficult with houses of worship due to the intricacies of construction, yet this method can provide reliable results that are similar to the other methods when properly applied.

On occasion the services of a specialist or contractor may be required to estimate the cost new for a religious facility. Contractors and architects are excellent sources of cost new data.

Following are examples of cost new estimates along with samples of how to present these data. Some discussion is provided as to what might be included or omitted from a particular cost source.

Actual Costs

When provided with actual "total" cost new, it is important to determine if the following items were included: site value, site improvements, and landscaping; direct costs including performance bonds, permits, builders profit (as opposed to entrepreneurial profit) and overhead, all interior finish, pews, stained glass, architectural features such as domes and steeples, sound systems, and video equipment; and indirect costs including civil and structural engineering, accounting, appraisal, and legal fees, carrying costs and taxes on the land (vacant land owned by a nonprofit is sometimes taxed until improved), financing fees, points and interest on the construction and permanent or takeout loan, title policy, and any other legitimate costs.

Appraisers should note that these figures are often provided in whole numbers and do not include all improvements or costs. Careful analysis of these figures is important since they are property specific with respect to difficult-to-estimate items including site improvements, site work, indirect costs, etc.

Indirect costs may or may not be included in the data provided. Even if dated, this information can be useful with the help of cost indexing. Cost indexing simply involves dividing the current cost index for a particular area by the historical cost index and multiplying the result by the historical cost. Care must be taken that the indexing is accurate. When indexing costs, it is sometimes helpful to call the actual contractor to find out how much costs have changed since the project was completed. Obviously, this would be a reproduction cost estimate and site/property specific. Typically, these costs are provided either as a lump sum or on a per-square-foot basis. In some cases a very detailed contractor's breakdown is available.

FIGURE 1: Actual Cost Estimate for a Religious Facility

	Per Square Foot
General and administrative	$0.56
Professional expenses	8.58
Construction expenses	
Site work	0.78
Demolition/cleaning	0.14
Earthwork	0.24
Drilled footings	0.07
Landscaping	0.36
Concrete	0.55
Forms	0.27
Reinforcing steel	0.13
Masonry	2.90
Stone	0.16
Precast panels	0.14
Structural steel	1.58
Miscellaneous metals/access panels	1.43
Ornamental metals	0.49
Steel stairs	1.05
Scaffolding	0.20
Carpentry	0.53
Millwork	3.44
Light weight deck	0.19
Roofing and sheet metal	2.44
Waterproofing	0.24
Hollow metal	0.20
Finish hardware	0.58
Glass and aluminium	1.80
Wood doors	0.28
Special doors	0.30
Lathe/plaster	2.47
Drywall	6.04
Ceramic/tile/pavers	1.57
Painting/wall covering	1.02
Accoustical tile	0.89
Vinyl base and carpet	1.75
Wood floors/insulation/track	0.73
Toilet partitions	0.18
Miscellaneous floors—special	0.36
Special equipment	1.36
Art glass	1.21
Elevators	0.23
Fire protection	0.48
Mechanical	9.51
Electrical	5.98
General conditions	1.66
Permits/bonds/builders' risk	0.47
Miscellaneous labor	0.20
Contractor's fee	2.66
Testing	0.23
Miscellaneous	0.59
Total per square foot	$69.21

The above costs do not include interest during construction, points, appraisal fees, closing costs, legal and administrative, or other indirect costs.

Sometimes actual costs are provided via a contractor's format. An example of an actual contractor's cost format appears in Figure 1.

Cost Comparables

Using cost comparable information provides an excellent check on the reasonableness of other methods of developing cost new. As special-use properties are often custom built, with very different building standards and differing quality, it is not unusual for there to be a wide cost variance between facilities. Nonetheless, when analyzed carefully, similar facilities typically will have a similar cost new, subject to the occasional aberration.

Figure 2 illustrates a write-up of a cost comparable. Costs will vary significantly depending on quality of construction, ratio of sanctuary space to total area, ceiling heights, percent of peripheral space, site improvements, and numerous other issues. Photographs are helpful in ascertaining the comparability to the subject.

A summary similar to that found in Figure 2 is not unusual. The appraiser should develop and rely on those cost comparables *most similar* to the subject. In some cases someone at the facility will have been the building coordinator or business manager at the time of construction and may be able to answer questions about actual costs. It is imperative that these data be analyzed carefully. What was actually included in the costs? Were any unusual site, utility, permit, or other costs noted? Were any materials or labor donated? Was this an addition or an original facility? How large is the sanctuary relative to the total area built? Sanctuaries are typically more expensive to build than classroom space. Was the

---

FIGURE 2: Religious Facility Cost Comparable

Date of Cost Bid/Construction:	One year ago
Name of Facility:	First Church
Location:	Amherst and Caroline
Items included:	All site improvements, pews, kitchen equipment, stained glass, sound system and speakers, builder's profit and overhead, architectural fees, and indirect costs.
Description of Improvements:	A 16,000-sq.-ft. religious facility with fixed seating for 320 persons with an average ceiling height of 18 feet. The exterior is all brick, the roof is pitched, and the interior has carpeted floors, dropped ceilings, and fluorescent overhead lighting. The construction was developed with a performance bond. Indirect costs included 1 point construction/permanent loan fees, nominal taxes on the land, legal fees, and parkland fees.
Cost New:	$69.72 per sq. ft.

---

facility built by a licensed or bonded contractor? Inspecting cost comparables, in particular those relied upon, is prudent.

It may be necessary to select an alternative cost comparable for specific portions of a facility that may be different from a typical facility. These might include a day-care facility, a classroom or school building, or a retail facility. *In any event, expanding on the conclusion reached is imperative.* Relying on cost comparables is recommended only where the costs can be reliably confirmed and if the facilities are very similar, have similar sites, and were built during a similar time frame.

Cost Services

As might be expected, in very stable areas or where no new construction has occurred, it is reasonable to use cost data from other regions and adjust them for location. Most cost service data can be adjusted for different areas of the country.

Numerous cost services exist for special-use properties. Most base their information on actual costs and/or bids from contractors and adjust figures for different locations and time. The first and most important item to consider when using a cost service is to properly categorize the subject facility. Most facilities lend themselves well to the descriptions in the cost manuals. Some facilities, however, are so specialized that they defy a "blanket" category such as "church or religious facility" found in cost service materials. In such cases the building may be divided into its relevant portions and separate cost estimates developed for such components as the sanctuary, classrooms, day care, restaurants/kitchens, nursing homes, apartments, and administrative offices. This technique can be useful in estimating the cost new for more elaborate, ornate, and diverse facilities. Items specific to the subject including stained glass, pews, ceiling heights, bell towers, etc., typically must be analyzed separately. Perimeter multipliers and ceiling heights are often an important part of the analysis because religious facilities can have very high ceilings/roofs, with very irregular shapes, which normally add to the cost.

Whether using actual costs, cost comparables, or a cost service to develop cost new, one of these will generally arise as the most reliable and should be supported by the other methods. At this point, the appraiser has to ascertain the degree of confidence he or she places in the cost new estimate. The balance of the report and the resulting value conclusions will key off in part from the cost new. Erroneous data at this point could seriously undermine the balance and thus the reliability of the report.

Although other sources of cost new exist, they are rarely utilized. These include a contractor's estimate, which can be costly if bid out on an item-by-item basis. Some contractors will provide a "general estimate" based on a project they may have recently completed. Architects often have a reasonable estimate of the cost new for a given facility. An architect intimately familiar with a given facility can provide excellent insight into the cost new. For new construction, it is imperative to receive the contractor's bid estimates for the facility. In most cases, the facility should be working with more than one contractor, and in these cases it is suggested that all bid estimates be presented.

Few if any religious facilities are built with a profit incentive. Therefore, the inclusion of entrepreneurial profit is generally inappropriate. In fact, by definition, most religious facilities are "nonprofit" and need to remain so to continue to obtain certain benefits. As such, a profit incentive is generally inappropriate to the cost new. On the other hand, contractor's reasonable overhead and profit should be included as a cost. An additional factor that frequently arises is donated labor or materials. Such items must be carefully analyzed if they are to be included as a cost.

In conclusion, the estimated cost new is a pivotal point in the valuation of a religious facility and must be analyzed carefully. An error in this section of the report will follow the valuation process through the final value estimate. Careful inspections, coupled with a multifaceted estimate of cost new, will help alleviate cost new issues and add reliability to the final value estimate.

DEPRECIATION

The estimation of depreciation within the cost approach will trigger an additional series of calculations that will often pervade the balance of the report. In this section it is imperative to identify not only the physical curable, physical long-lived, and physical short-lived items but also the functional and external items, if any.

Physical Deterioration

The physical age/effective physical age of a facility is paramount to a discussion of physical depreciation. Religious facilities are often overused because they are open to the public. That is to say, many facilities offer numerous events which attract large numbers of people. Even if properly maintained, a facility with such constant use may indicate an "effective physical age" that is greater than the chronological age or weighted average chronological age. On the other hand a facility that is only used for one weekly service and one evening for education programs will typically have an effective physical age/condition that is less than the chronological age. This factor is generally at the discretion of the appraiser, but should be based in part on the actual chronological age with appropriate adjustments.

Physical curable depreciation of both short-lived and long-lived building components must be accounted for, which includes items that a prudent purchaser/owner would cure. Most religious groups take pride in their facilities, yet some suffer from "overuse" or atypical wear and tear. Generally, however, the members will not allow physical curable depreciation to become unreasonable. Members often find it fulfilling to donate a roof or HVAC system when needed, and thus extensive deferred maintenance is unusual.

Short-lived components consist of the items whose lives are less than the shell. Typically these include the roof, HVAC system (or a portion of), plumbing and electrical fixtures, interior finish/painting, and wall and floor coverings (these can be extensive and very short-lived). Other short-lived items include decorative or functional elements incidental to the operation (pew seat covers, baptistery, etc.), extensive kitchen equipment if included, PA systems, paving, and possibly landscaping. The lives of short-lived items vary depending on location, quality of original equipment/item, etc. Some religious facilities are constructed with commercial-grade materials and others are built with residential-grade components, which can greatly influence the lives of these items. The appraiser must be careful to properly analyze the total life and effective physical age of the component.

The long-lived portions of buildings—generally the shell—vary greatly depending on the type of construction and the area of the country in which the facility exists. Usually this factor is developed as the cost new less the short-lived items, both adjusted for any curable depreciation as appropriate. Therefore, by comparing the effective (physical) age of the shell with the estimated total physical or total useful life, the total physical depreciation applicable to the long-lived items can be segregated. This methodology is preferred because religious facilities/special-use properties obtain much of their desirability/utility from their physical condition.

Determining the effective (physical) age and the total useful (physical) life of the property is central to the process. The effective physical age is typically a function of the maintenance of the property and may correspond to the actual age. Depending on the upkeep of the property, effective (physical) age can be best estimated from the reference point of actual age. In the case of a campus facility, with buildings of different ages, the effective age for each structure is estimated, from which a weighted average effective physical age for the entire complex can be developed. Total physical or useful life is obviously more difficult to determine and needs to be a function of the quality of construction and durability of the shell components. Total physical lives of 30 years to well over 100 years are not unusual.

Functional Obsolescence

Relative to religious facilities, functional obsolescence is often the inability of a particular facility to properly fulfill the needs of a "typical" user/buyer in the market. This may include a need for extensive seating or support facilities, numerous education wings, more than one kitchen, buildings that face a certain direction, etc. It is recognized that most buyers of used religious facilities have particular needs that are tied to their particular beliefs. Most congregations would probably like something that is different from what may be available in the "used religious facility market." This is why so many groups build exactly what they want and need. It is the appraiser's job to determine if a facility is "generally functional to support the needs of a typical congregation" in the market in which the facility exists. For a facility not to suffer from what appraisers refer to as functional obsolescence, items necessary for the proper and adequate operation of the facility, based on requirements of the local market of buyers and users, must be present.

Parking is often noted as a functional issue. It is not unusual for a religious facility to operate functionally yet have insufficient parking. Factors to consider regarding parking are whether or not a problem can be readily alleviated or cured as well as whether or not parking is a factor with the congregants, is legal, and is affecting the operations of the facility. Many religious organizations need extensive parking only on Saturday or Sunday mornings or one or more evenings a week. Frequently local businesses agree to lease or donate some of their parking during these periods. In some cases parking at a school, park, large parking garage, or open lot or on-street parking is available to compensate for lack of on-site parking. The parking issue is another reason that religious facilities prefer to buy "excess land" when they are looking for a site. If the parking issue cannot be overcome, it is likely a functional problem. Lack of parking, maybe even more than lack of sanctuary seating, could limit the size of the congregation that could use the facility. Other parking issues pertain to zoning requirements and local codes. A detailed discussion on parking requirements appeared in a previous chapter on the physical facility. If parking is inadequate, even if it is in conformity with local codes, this issue could be functional obsolescence and must be addressed.

A group buying an existing religious facility may desire one that is similar to yet not exactly like the one available in the market. Technically this appears to be a functional issue, yet it is very congregation specific. Seldom is there a buyer in the market looking for exactly what is available in the "used religious facility" market. As such, buyers often insist on a discount over physical deterioration to account for changes they will make to the facility to fulfill *their* needs.

Measuring more typical functional obsolescence is difficult at best. Often a cost to cure will solve a rest room or parking problem if there is excess land (functional curable). In cases where no additional space or rest rooms can be added (utility capacity, etc.), this would likely represent a functional incurable situation. The measurement of these factors is significantly more difficult. It is not unusual to see functional superadequacy in a facility built by a particular congregation that is more than what the market is willing to pay for. More often the original congregation built exactly what it needed or desired, and a potential buyer is simply looking for something different or in a slightly different location. Other functional issues relate to the construction of the facility (oversized foundations, excess ceiling heights, etc.), which can often be eliminated by using replacement cost rather than reproduction cost in the cost approach.

External Obsolescence

In commercial property, external or economic obsolescence is typically associated with conditions or factors external to the property—for example, an area suffering from an extensive economic downturn or a location next to an adverse influence. In some cases, these typical and readily identifiable items can be a factor with religious facilities, but often a market-based obsolescence factor comes into play with these properties. It is often difficult to differentiate if the depreciation in excess of physical is due to buyer preferences (functional) or due to economic conditions (external). Nonetheless, the measurement of depreciation in excess of physical deterioration must be accounted for and typically can be extracted from market data.

THE MARKET EXTRACTION METHOD

This discussion of depreciation thus far has focused on factors that are property-specific rather than stem from lack of demand, an economic downturn, or changes in preferences for facilities. The following discussion will develop depreciation from the market and will offer some suggestions for dealing with depreciation in excess of physical deterioration and a suggested methodology for estimating depreciation in a given market.

It is not unusual for all sales in a given market to suffer from depreciation in excess of physical deterioration, whether it be functional (due to the existing facilities being different from those desired by buyers) or external (from market conditions). Regardless of cause, it must be accounted for. An extraction grid (see Figure 3) can be helpful in determining the total accrued depreciation influencing a particular property.

A great deal of information can be garnered from preparing such a grid if properly developed. The analysis can determine if in fact buyers are willing to pay the physically depreciated cost for facilities in a given market. In some cases where demand is high, buyers are sometimes willing to pay more than the depreciated cost of a facility, due to the difficulty of development, time issues, development moratoriums, or other demand/supply issues.

The total economic life can be estimated along with the total depreciation rate of the improvements. The total yearly depreciation becomes useful in determining the rate at which a facility appears to be deteriorating (in total) per year and if and/or when an alternative use may be indicated as the highest and best use. Often the yearly depreciation factors are relatively similar among facilities, in particular when their ages are similar and/or when effective (physical) ages approximate actual ages.

The first factor to consider in this analysis is the site value of each sale, which will require the development of a "mini-appraisal" for each site. This can be accomplished through conversations with local brokers as well as with data on comparable sales, listings, the purchase price of the sale site if recent, and other reasonable techniques that are available. In many cases, the facilities are located in areas where no recent sales have occurred and no listings exist. All sites may be occupied, in which case a land residual technique may be the most appropriate methodology. When a facility is located in a residential area and is zoned residential, often its highest and best use as vacant is residential; thus, value is tied to the value of residential lots in the area, which may only be developed via a land residual technique. A reasonable determination of the land value is imperative to develop a depreciation extraction grid properly.

The next factor to consider is the total cost new of the sale. It is important to be consistent in the application of replacement cost or reproduction cost. All sales should be made cash equivalent and adjusted for conditions of sale. Obviously, a careful inspection of the sale facility is necessary. For consistency, it is necessary to use the same source for cost new for each sale so the results of the extraction are not skewed due to factors particular to a given sale. In this analysis it is necessary to effectively develop the total cost new, includ-

FIGURE 3: Extraction of Total Depreciation from the Comparable Sales

	Sale No. 1	Sale No. 2	Sale No. 3	Sale No. 4
Sale price	$370,000	$472,277	$1,985,217	$800,000
Size of facility/sq. ft.	4,700	11,000	51,454	25,000
Sale price/sq. ft.	$78.72	$42.93	$38.58	$32.00
Seating	N/A	320	1,500	550
Land area/acres	3.19	1.508	5	1.6
Land value/sq. ft	$0.80	$0.50	$0.50	$0.55
Total estimated land value	$111,165	$32,844	$108,900	$38,333
Indicated contributory value of improvements	$258,835	$439,433	$1,876,317	$761,667
Contributory value of improvements only/sq. ft.	$55.07	$39.95	$36.47	$30.47
Estimated total cost new/sq. ft.	$67.50	$55.00	$45.00	$65.00
Estimated total cost new	$317,250	$605,000	$2,315,430	$1,625,000
Total indicated depreciation	$58,415	$165,567	$439,113	$863,333
Indicated total depreciation as a %	18%	27%	19%	53%
Actual physical (chronological) age	15 yrs.	15 yrs.	10 yrs.	35 yrs.
Effective physical age	10 yrs.	15 yrs.	10 yrs.	35 yrs.
Total estimated physical life	75 yrs.	75 yrs.	75 yrs.	75 yrs.
Indicated physical depreciation	13%	20%	13%	47%
Functional depreciation	0%	0%	0%	0%
External depreciation*	5%	7%	6%	6%
Yearly depreciation based on effective age	1.84%	1.82%	1.90%	1.52%
Yearly depreciation based on physical age	1.23%	1.82%	1.90%	1.52%
Indicated total economic life	54 yrs.	55 yrs.	53 yrs.	66 yrs.

* Depreciation in excess of physical

Total depreciation per year

High	1.90%
Low	1.52%
Mean	1.77%

ing all factors, for each of the sales. Items that are often overlooked include excessive site work, parking areas, extensive fixtures or stained glass, and indirect costs. Additionally, since the cost new of each of the facilities could conceivably be used in the sales comparison approach for a quality adjustment, it is imperative that the relationship between each of the sales is consistent.

After deducting the estimated site value from the price of each sale, the balance remaining is the depreciated cost or contributory value of the improvements; i.e., what a typical buyer would be willing to pay for the improvements only. Next the contributory value of the improvements is deducted from the estimated total cost new (as of the date of the sale) to develop the total depreciation that has occurred. The difference is the total depreciation (physical, functional, and external) that has occurred to the improvements.

To determine if depreciation in excess of physical deterioration is occurring in a given market or to a given sale, as a check of reasonableness, the physical components may be further broken out, typically on the basis of the effective (physical) age/total useful (physical) life method. Other methods are available to determine the total physical depreciation. Care should be taken to be consistent in estimating the total physical depreciation from each of the sales. By comparing the estimated total depreciation with the estimated total physical depreciation, depreciation in excess of physical, if any, can be estimated. If there is depreciation in excess of physical deterioration, it must be analyzed and measured, although in some cases it is difficult to determine its exact cause.

If the contributory value of the improvements is more than the total depreciated cost or the physically depreciated cost, it indicates a buyer was willing to pay a premium over the depreciated cost of the improvement. Although this is not typical, it is also not unusual, particularly when a group desires to be in a given area or has found a facility that completely fulfills its exact needs. Consider, for example, an existing facility that has the authority via zoning/deed restrictions to operate a school, day-care center, or other peripheral support operation in an area where permits for such uses are not currently available.

In many markets, the total depreciation is in excess of physical deterioration. This is to be expected as almost every religious facility is built for a specific user as of a specific time period. As times change and as congregations grow or contract, the "contributory value" of the improvements changes for the owner as well as for a potential buyer. In any given market, the needs of the community vary over time. In many communities, a religious facility is simply a Sunday place of worship with a large sanctuary, a few administrative offices, and classrooms that more than fulfill the needs of the community. On the other hand, in large urban areas of the country, there is a definite need for expansive or "mega" religious facilities, providing schools, day care, elderly care, homeless shelters, soup kitchens, etc., for the community. The appraiser has to carefully analyze the market in which a facility exists or in which one is proposed to determine if it is consistent with the needs of the community.

In some cases depreciation in excess of physical depreciation is due to other factors.

As mentioned earlier, in many cases the facility that is purchased is not exactly what the purchasers would have built for themselves. This is likely a functional issue. An economic downturn in the community is more likely external obsolescence. Other external factors which may influence depreciation in excess of physical are more typical, such as being in an area that is noisy (airplane traffic during a service, trains, etc.). More rare is the stigma associated with a facility where a crime or other heinous event occurred.

In analyzing the conclusions of the market extraction of depreciation, it should first be determined if the market is willing to pay the depreciated cost for facilities. If so, there appears to be a reasonable need for facilities that are typical for the area. If there is some functional or external obsolescence in excess of physical depreciation, additional analysis may be necessary. Discussions with local brokers, building committee members, or the business managers of the purchased facilities can help identify the exact issues. Additionally, if there are any new facilities being built, it is important to determine how they differ from what is available in the "used facility" market. This should help determine why buyers are requiring a "discount" or paying a premium in purchasing facilities.

In applying an external/functional (depreciation in excess of physical) factor to a religious facility, it is imperative to view the subject in light of the sales. Is it more or less functional than the sales? Is there a reason to believe that it is suffering from depreciation in excess of physical? Is the quality of the facility consistent with the needs and desires of the community?

Of additional interest is the rate of total depreciation occurring to the sales. When effective ages are similar, these factors tend to be very consistent. Additionally, this total yearly depreciation, when divided into 100%, provides an estimate of total economic life, or the term that the facility could reasonably provide utility to a typical user.

Once land value, a cost new estimate, an effective (physical) age (in some cases of curable, short- and long-lived items), and depreciation factors have been developed, the appraiser can begin the application and summary of the cost approach.

Example

Assume that a facility contains 10,000 square feet, is 15 years old, is in average condition for its age, and has a site value of $100,000. Assume many of the short-lived items have been updated or replaced over their lives, so that the effective (physical) age of the short-lived items is 10 years and the effective age of the long-lived items is consistent with the actual age, or 15 years.

Figure 4 provides a typical summary of the cost approach. Cost new was supplemented with costs for peripheral items that are not always included in the total costs from the contractor or national cost services.

Depreciation was first analyzed on the basis of the physical facility. Curable physical depreciation of $5,000 was assumed for the example. Short-lived items were estimated and depreciated on an age/life basis, after being reduced for the curable items (which are assumed to be cured). Obviously, in this case the short-lived items were assumed to have a

FIGURE 4: Cost Approach Summary

Estimated Cost New

Direct Costs

Building: 10,000 sq. ft. @ $60.00 / sq. ft.	$600,000
Site improvements: (paving / curbs / striping / lighting / landscaping / detention pond)	85,000
Pews: 250 lin. ft. @ $40.00 / lin. ft.	10,000
Stained glass: 50 sq. ft. @ $65.00 / sq. ft.	3,250
Sound system / speaker cluster	2,500
Total direct costs:	$700,750

Indirect Costs

Financing fees, legal, taxes during construction, appraisal fees and title work (assuming loan of $560,000 and .75% of a point or $4,200 for a combination construction loan and permanent loan), $2,500 legal, $2,000 in taxes on the site, $4,000 appraisal fee, and $1,500 for title policy   14,200

TOTAL ESTIMATED COST NEW $714,950

DEPRECIATION

Physical

Curable: Assume that this facility needs a new air conditioning and heating system—estimated cost new $5,000	$5,000

Incurable:

Short-lived: Assume $107,243 less curable items ($5,000) or $102,243 x 10 yrs. (effective physical age) / 25 yrs. (total physical life)	40,897
Long-lived: $607,708 x 15 yrs. (effective physical age) / 75 yrs. (total physical life)	121,542
Total estimated physical depreciation	$167,439

Functional

The subject facility appears to have typical functional attributes and does not suffer from any functional obsolescence.

External

The subject market appears to discount the sales of religious facilities, due to a recent economic downturn (market conditions). This factor has been estimated at 5% of the cost new from the depreciation extraction grid $35,748

Total estimated depreciation (28.42% or 1.9% / year)	$203,187
Depreciated value of the improvements	$511,763
Plus land value estimate	$100,000
Estimated value via the cost approach:	(rounded) $610,000

shorter effective physical age than the shell (because the short-lived items were well maintained and updated). The effective physical age of the shell was consistent with the actual age. Total physical life was estimated via conversations with contractors relative to the total physical life of typical components along with several facilities whose physical life approximated 75 years. As a test of reasonableness, the concluded depreciation for the subject of 28.42%, or 1.89% per year, is consistent on the high side with the depreciation occurring per year for the sales (1.23% to 1.9% per year). As an alternative, the yearly depreciation indicated for the subject could be construed at the upper end of the range or 1.9% times an age of 15 years or 28.5% (total indicated depreciation).

The depreciation base for the long-lived items (the shell) was estimated as the difference between the short-lived items and the total cost. The long-lived items were depreciated at the actual/effective physical age of the shell.

No functional obsolescence was noted. The obsolescence noted in the depreciation extraction grid was labeled external as it appeared universal in the market, based on the market extraction of depreciation. The external depreciation noted in the extraction grid ranged generally from 5% to 7%. A factor of 5% represents a reasonable external obsolescence in excess of physical depreciation, based on the above noted analysis. For the purposes of the example it is assumed that the area has undergone a slight economic downturn.

By deducting total depreciation from the cost new estimate, the depreciated cost, or contributory value of the improvements, is indicated. The land value must be added to this factor.

In conclusion, by extracting total depreciation through this analysis, buyers' perceptions of properties are integrated into the cost approach. This methodology, in part, removes the cost approach's concept that cost equals value. Thus, so long as sales are available, a reliable estimate of value may be developed. If applied properly, items such as the demand for facilities can be brought into the equation via the selection (based on reason/market facts) of the excess depreciation factors, if any. In some markets where activity is nominal, it is common for depreciation in excess of physical deterioration to be extensive. This brings the demand side of the equation into the cost approach. By bringing the local sales data into the estimate of depreciation, the value estimate via the cost approach should parallel how market participants are viewing the value of properties.

Chapter Seven
THE SALES COMPARISON APPROACH

Comparable sales are more rare to find when valuing special-use properties than more typical property types. For religious facilities, nonetheless, a relatively well-defined market exists in most markets throughout the United States. Sales do occur in most areas. In fact, there appears to be a relatively well-organized group of professionals who serve this market. Sources of data at the national and/or local level include:

- Bankers active in lending to religious facilities

- Church financiers and broker-dealers

- Real estate brokers who specialize in religious facilities

- Contractors

- Architects

- Professional clergy

- Religious administrators or business managers

- Organizations of religious groups or church administrators

Tapping this cadre of professionals is paramount to developing a reliable and thorough sales comparison approach.

A search for sales needs to start with the subject's physical characteristics. If the subject consists of a 7,000-square-foot one-room facility, a local search for sales probably needs to be developed. If, however, the subject is a 250,000-square-foot facility with a sanctuary seating 4,000, a school, cafeteria, nursing home, and numerous other enhancing features, a national search for comparables is recommended, with support from the local market.

In addition to the typical information gathered in the sales comparison approach for any type of property (i.e., date of sale, buyer/seller, conditions of sale, land area, zoning, etc.), the following items are relevant to religious facilities: sanctuary description and seating capacity, ratio of total building area per seat, potential for expansion, and reasons for selling or buying.

Once the sales have been chosen, the comparison process begins. Unless the data are very comparable, it is suggested that the land value be extracted from each of the sale(s) to be able to compare the contributory value of the improvements. This is similar to a process sometimes used for industrial properties. In doing so, most locational adjustments are eliminated (assuming that land value accounts for the quality of the location), and land-to-building ratios are accounted for, as are variances in site sizes and values. The sale prices per square foot, per cubic foot, or per pew, etc., can then be compared to that of the subject.

Generally, comparisons on the basis of price per square foot of improvements are most useful for religious facilities. Nonetheless, religious facilities can be compared on a per pew or per seat basis, although the price per pew or seat is reliable only if the ratios of the total building area per seat are similar. When they are not, a given seat is supporting more or less peripheral space. Although adjustments for this factor can be developed, this methodology is considered only marginally reliable where differences in the ratio of seating to total building areas are expanding. In some cases this factor can be accounted for by multiplying the indicated value per seat/pew for each sale by the ratio of the comparable sale seating to the subject's total area. This is similar to adjusting apartment projects (analyzed on a per unit basis) for average unit size.

Developing a reliable land value estimate for the comparables is paramount to the application of this analysis. This is imperative to extract depreciation in the cost approach. It is suggested that one or more land sales or listings located in proximity to each comparable sale be used, supplemented by conversations with a broker/appraiser or property owner familiar with the area. Optimally it would be best to appraise the land under each comparable sale separately. This is done on occasion but typically it is impractical to perform. Nonetheless, the reliability of the depreciation extraction is very sensitive to land value estimates.

It is typical to align the sales by date of sale from most recent to oldest. As with most single-purpose or special-use properties, the comparability of the data is typically not as close as with more common types of properties. If several very similar sales are available, a grid can be developed showing adjustments for the nominal variations. For the vast majority of cases, the following suggested analysis will serve more easily to adjust the sales to the subject. Numerous variations are possible and sometimes necessary depending on the issues occurring in the market and the data available.

It is suggested that each sale be adjusted for conditions of sale and financing within the sale write-up, so that the extraction of depreciation analysis is more similar for each sale. Thus, when aligned, the sales will reflect the sale prices per square foot of building area only, adjusted for condition of sale and cash equivalency.

At this point it is necessary to analyze the specific sales to determine if they are similar enough to compare on an item-by-item basis (with or without land). That is to say, is the depth of the market sufficient to compare sales on an item-by-item basis (e.g., design and appeal, quality, size, location, age/condition, seating ratios, etc.)? This is generally rare. More typically the available sales are at first glance only nominally comparable and likely were sold in widely varying locales.

As most comparable sales of religious facilities are very different physically and subject to different neighborhood influences, their comparison becomes more difficult. To account for vastly different physical facilities, amenities, qualities, and locations, it is necessary for the appraiser to take a broader view of their comparability.

The following discussion of some adjustments provides suggestions for applying them in the valuation process. This is meant to serve as a template from which to begin the appraisal process of a religious facility. Numerous variations on this same theme obviously exist.

ADJUSTMENTS

Conditions of sale

Conditions of sale tend to be unique in religious facilities. Often a group that needs to expand or contract its facility finds "exactly what it needs" and is willing to pay significantly more than anyone else in the market. This situation becomes particularly germane when land sales are discussed. Practically by definition, religious facilities are locationally sensitive. If a congregation wants to expand its facility, it typically is very limited with respect to the area it can move to and retain its membership. Thus, a facility or site in its "market area" may be worth far more to them than the sales might indicate.

Obviously, from time to time a facility is exactly what the congregation needs. This condition of sale is difficult to determine and typically shows up as an aberrated sale price. The congregation's decision makers can shed significant light on the building committee's decision process. The purpose of many appraisal assignments is to determine how much a given congregation can pay for a facility and not pay more than the market value.

A common condition of sale for religious groups occurs when a congregation purchases a facility located very near or abutting its existing facility. Because the process of building a new facility is difficult, expensive, and very time consuming, the congregation may be willing to purchase an existing facility for significantly more than its depreciated cost plus the value of its land. It is obviously assumed that the purchaser has a need for more or different space. Measuring this particular condition of sale often requires a combination of conversations with the decision makers of the facility coupled with common sense as to how much more the congregation could conceivably spend before the build-to-suit alternative (new) overshadows the cost of the existing (used) facility. The opposite often occurs when a nearby or abutting facility becomes available and is purchased "just in case it is needed" or because the "price was right." In these cases, the congregation was enticed into purchasing the facility.

Numerous other items come into play with respect to conditions of sale. These might include stigma effect from environmental problems or heinous crimes committed in or near the facilities as well as serious problems with leadership. Careful confirmation of the data coupled with an analysis of the local market will help alleviate the possibility of missing a condition of sale adjustment.

Financing

It is not unusual for religious facilities to sell with unusual financing, making this factor important to analyze carefully. Often an existing group will assist a new or growing organization by financing a facility. Items that are typical and require adjustment include insufficient down payment, a below-market interest rate, facilities that are leased with the lease payments applied to a down payment, trades, and "soft seconds." Several religious groups finance their facilities with advantageous financing and/or "soft seconds" for the down payments. Sales that occur under these situations must be analyzed carefully. Typical cash equivalent financing analysis is suggested.

Market Conditions (Time)

Market conditions are a very relevant factor in the valuation of religious facilities. Quite obviously, the most accurate accounting of this factor is via paired sales; however, sales of religious facilities are difficult and rare enough to find without expecting to find two sales of the same religious facility over a reasonable time period. What makes this adjustment even more difficult is that religious facilities often grow during economic downturns or in times of crisis. As such, simply measuring the general economic activity can be deceiving. A careful analysis of the regional and local economies, along with the needs for facilities, can help determine if values have been changing over time. Questions to answer include:

- Are facilities sitting for sale for over 12 months with no activity?

- Is there an abundance of facilities "for sale" (listed or otherwise)?

- Are there many sales in the area/region?

- Is there significant new construction or additions occurring in the area/region?

- Is the area in a growth mode (population, employment, etc.)?

- Do some facilities have more than one offer at the same time?

- Are land/site values decreasing or increasing?

If only a few sites are available for religious facility construction, and there is an active sales market, some appreciation may be occurring. On the other hand, if there are numerous facilities on the market with few users/offers, this could indicate that values are declining. The average marketing period is a reasonable indicator of what is occurring in the market.

At this juncture, the analysis has focused only on the contributory value of the improvements, and little consideration has been given to the site. Nonetheless, it would appear reasonable to assume that the direction of site values is an indication of market activity and demand for property in general. Obviously, land values can be tracked through more typical methodology. While it is possible for land and improvement values to move in opposite directions, this is unlikely.

Location

It is recognized that improvements in a superior location often contribute more value than a similar facility in an undesirable location. By eliminating the land value from the sale, location is typically accounted for in most cases. This factor can be similarly accounted for in the selection of the final value per square foot and/or leaning toward the upper or lower limit of the range, depending on the circumstances. That is to say, if the location of the subject is very desirable, it would appear reasonable to assume that the site value would be equally desirable/valuable. As such, a conclusion near the upper end of the value range might be appropriate.

Items that appear relevant to the location of a religious facility include the following:

- Do the typical members have reasonable access to the location?

- Is the location a recognizable property address?

- Is the site easily visible from a major roadway?

- Is the facility consistent with the area's needs (consistent use)?

- Is the neighborhood growing, declining, or stable?

Obviously, numerous other items with respect to location can be adjusted and/or noted.

Size

Size adjustments in religious facilities can be atypical of the rule of thumb that larger facilities generally sell for less per square foot than equally similar smaller facilities. This is frequently not the case with religious facilities. In particular, it is not unusual for very large and newer facilities, which are very ornate and include numerous peripheral items, to sell for more per square foot than otherwise dramatic smaller facilities. This is likely due to the propensity of buyers to only look for a facility in their need range, plus a little for growth.

Contractors may contradict that it costs less per square foot to construct 100,000 square feet than 20,000 square feet, all other things being equal. The contradiction appears explained in that most facilities are so different. Any two religious facilities normally differ significantly with respect to ceiling heights, quality, amenities, interior finish, stained glass, built-in items, and the like.

Thus, it is unusual to make a size adjustment for religious facilities. An exception to this would be a facility that was substantially overbuilt for a given market; this, however, is more likely a functional superadequacy than a situation requiring a true size adjustment. It would be considered generally inappropriate in a typical appraisal to use the sale of a 100,000-square-foot facility when the subject was 20,000 square feet. But in the case of a nonprofit or special-use facility, there are cases where the only and/or best sale may be one that appears vastly different yet is fulfilling similar needs in the community. Thus, it could be reasonably comparable if the buyers have similar needs, expectations, and desires.

Quality

Quality, as much as any factor, must be analyzed carefully. When in doubt bring in an expert (e.g., architect, contractor, cost estimator) to properly ascertain the quality of a particular facility. There are numerous facilities of average quality yet their manner of design or construction can be deceptive. Examples include painted glass or plastic windows instead of stained or faceted glass, and metal buildings with brick facades versus brick exteriors with steel framing. Other items that can be deceiving are roof composition, roof lines, energy efficiency, steeple heights, perimeter complexity, framing, and stained glass. These items must be carefully ascertained for both the subject and the comparables. In some markets, excess quality is not accounted for by buyers. To some buyers a brick facade is equal to a brick-framed building. In such a case, the adjustment for quality might need to be qualified.

In this analysis, it is suggested that the appraiser compare the subject's cost new (actual or estimated) with the total estimated cost new for the particular comparable sale. Paramount to making adjustments for quality are reliable cost new estimates for the comparable sales and the subject. Cost new is critical in developing a reliable value estimate since many factors key off of this figure. Thus, care must be taken in developing cost new estimates and in any subsequent adjustments. For example, this analysis could be developed as follows:

Sale total cost new	$ 60.00/sq. ft.
Subject total cost new	$ 70.00/sq. ft.
Difference	$ 10.00/sq. ft.

Assuming that the market recognizes a dollar-for-dollar difference, this analysis would indicate a +16.67% adjustment to the sale for its inferior quality as compared to the subject. It must be carefully determined if the market in which the subject exists recognizes the additional quality of the subject in total. This is likely best determined by the quality of current construction and current sales and ultimately by whether buyers are willing to pay for additional quality. Some markets simply want size and/or function and are not concerned with quality. In fact, in some congregations, excess quality could be considered undesirable due to their religious beliefs. In other markets, congregations are very interested in worshiping in facilities that are of high quality or consistent with how they live. All these factors must be considered in determining how best to apply this adjustment.

It is recognized that this adjustment implies that the cost equals value, which is often not the case. Nonetheless, all other things being equal, a typical buyer of a religious facility would likely desire more rather than less quality. The appraiser's job is to determine at what point a typical buyer would not pay more for more quality.

Age/Condition (Total Depreciation)

Adjustments for age and condition have been combined here because these items are directly related with respect to *total* depreciation. That is to say, in the extraction of depreciation analysis previously described, the contributory value of the improvements was extracted leading to the development of *total* depreciation. All physical depreciation, functional obsolescence, and external/economic depreciation would be included. This adjustment therefore compares the contributory value of the improvements of the sales to that of the subject. The suggested adjustment for this factor is based on the following formula:

$$\frac{(1 - \text{total depreciation of the subject}) - (1 - \text{total depreciation of the sale})}{(1 - \text{Total depreciation of the sale})}$$

By using this formula, a "percent good" of the subject is compared with a "percent good" of the sale and adjusted accordingly. This analysis can provide large adjustments. Nonetheless, in special-use, single-purpose facilities that can differ significantly, often the only sales are vastly different with respect to age, condition, and functional and/or external obsolescence. With this analysis, such sales can be compared reasonably and quantitatively.

Other adjustments could be developed, yet by adjusting for quality, *all* physical dissimilarities are accounted for. Additionally, by adjusting for depreciation as noted above, *all* depreciation is accounted for. In some cases it might be appropriate to only include an adjustment for physical items and separate out external/functional issues. The critical element is to account for the issues influencing the subject property.

There are numerous other factors which tend to avail themselves to appraisers for adjustment purposes. These include stigma factors, facilities that sell as aberrations due to their unusual desirability (views, historical significance, etc.). Additionally, design and appeal are issues that are difficult at best to value.

The following case study provides some suggested methodologies for developing a sales comparison approach. Much of the information presented was taken from actual sale data.

DIRECT SALES COMPARISON APPROACH— CASE STUDY

The subject is a 10,000-square-foot brick veneer religious facility with a site value of $100,000, a cost new of $71.50 per square foot, and total depreciation of 28.42% (see Figure 3, extraction of depreciation grid, on page 45).

The following analysis of sales was made to make allowances for dissimilar characteristics in relation to the subject property. The analysis was based on price per square foot rather than price per pew or seat because they are not considered appropriate in the subject market.

The land-to-building ratios varied greatly for the improved sales. Therefore, the land values for the comparable sales were estimated and deducted from the sale prices to arrive at the contributory value of the improvements. This was considered to be the appropriate method of analyzing the comparable sales in relation to the subject. This analysis was also necessary to extract the total depreciation in the cost approach.

SALE NO. 1:

Key Map:	251D
Date of Sale:	Current (on the market eight months)
Property Location:	18 Mill Road
Grantor:	Living Word Church
Grantee:	Church A
Legal Description:	3.19 acres out of the Any County School Land Survey
Recording Data:	Deed 2135
Price:	$370,000
Per sq. ft.:	$78.72
Per sq. ft. - improvements only:	$55.07
Per seat:	N/A
Terms:	All cash
Land Area:	3.19 acres or 138,956 sq. ft.
Building Area:	4,700 sq. ft.
Land to Building Ratio:	29.57:1
Sanctuary Seating:	No fixed seating
Sq. ft. per seat:	N/A
Confirmed by:	Pastor Thomas
Description of Improvements:	This facility has adequate and conforming concrete parking for 100 cars, cedar exterior, average landscaping, tile and carpet flooring, no fixed seating, and a pitched composition shingle roof. The sellers have reported that a larger facility is needed to accommodate growing membership. This facility appears to be constructed of average quality materials and is in better than average condition for its age. The facility has an effective (physical) age of 10 years and an actual age of 15 years. The site value estimate was based on a recent sale of a similar tract in the same area for $0.80 per sq. ft. Cost new was based on the appraiser's calculation from a national cost service of the estimated cost new for the facility in total. The sale is a legally conforming use based on the local zoning ordinance.

SALE No. 2:

Key Map:	445 T
Date of Sale:	Six months ago (sold in 12 months)
Property Address / Location:	8809 Kirby
Grantor:	Southwest Bible Fellowship
Grantee:	First Philippine Church
Legal Description:	A 1.508 acre tract out of the Louis Survey, Abstract 1012.
Recording Data:	Film Code No. 171-65-1725
Cash Equivalent Sales Price:	$472,277
Per sq. ft.:	$42.93
Per sq. ft. - improvements only:	$39.95
Per seat:	$1,476
Terms:	The purchaser reportedly put $100,000 cash down (21%) and assumed a $272,277 mortgage due in 10 years with 9% interest and a 25-year amortization schedule. The difference of $100,000 was carried as a second by the seller, for five years at 9.75% - fully amortizing. Terms appear cash equivalent.
Land Area:	1.508 acres or 65,688 sq. ft.
Building Area:	11,000 sq. ft.
Land to Building Ratio:	5.97:1
Sanctuary Seating:	320
Sq. ft. per seat:	34 sq. ft.
Confirmed by:	Phil Mars, broker to the transaction
Land Description:	This is a level, 1.508-acre corner tract with frontage on Kirby and Glen Boulevard. All utilities were reported available at the site.
Description of Improvements:	This is an average quality religious facility in average condition for its age. It has a 7,000-sq.-ft. sanctuary (built 18 years ago) and a 4,000-sq.-ft. educational/kitchen area (built 10 years ago). The property is estimated to have an effective weighted average age of 15 years. Included in the sale were fixed seating for 320 persons, 14 classrooms, the podium, and limited kitchen appliances. Adequate and legally conforming parking is available on site. The land value estimate was based on a recent purchase of an abutting parcel by the facility. The cost new estimate was based on the seller's actual costs adjusted for time with support from a national cost survey.

SALE No. 3:

Date of Sale:	One year ago (sold in 13 months)
Property Address/Location:	7400 Ella
Property Name:	First West Church
Grantor:	First West Church
Grantee:	Best Ministries
Recording Data:	Film Code No. 182-79-1635
Reported Contract Sales Price:	$1,985,217
Cash Equivalent Sales Price:	$1,985,217
Per sq. ft.:	$38.58
Per sq. ft. - improvements only:	$36.47
Per seat:	$1,323
Terms:	Terms were reported as follows: $375,000 cash down with an additional $50,000 due in six months and secured by a letter of credit. Seller's financial institution reportedly offered the purchaser an assumption of the existing note of $1,560,217 at a market rate of 9.25% and a 10-year term, with a 20-year amortization schedule. Terms are generally considered cash equivalent.
Land Area:	5 acres or 217,800 sq. ft.
Building Area:	51,454 sq. ft.
Land to Building Ratio:	4.23
Sanctuary Seating:	1,500
Sq. ft. per seat:	34 sq. ft.
Confirmed by	Best Ministries pastor
Land Description:	This is a level five-acre tract of land. All utilities were reported available at the site. Frontage is adequate.
Description of Improvements:	This is a precast, tilt-wall-construction religious facility that appears to be in average condition for its age. The effective and actual age of the improvements is 10 years. The roof is pitched. The foundation is poured concrete, and the windows are casement. The interior finish includes carpeted and tile floors, sheetrock interior partitions, and fluorescent lighting. The building consists of two, two-story wings on both sides of a large sanctuary with a high beamed ceiling. Adequate parking appears available via on-site parking and a large park located directly across the street. The land value estimate of $0.50/sq. ft. is supported by a listing on the same block for $0.75/sq. ft., with the broker indicating that there have been several offers in the $0.50/sq. ft. range. The estimated cost new is based on the actual cost, adjusted for time, along with support from a national cost service.

SALE NO. 4:

Key Map:	666 E
Date of Sale:	Two years ago (sold in six months)
Property Address/Location:	700 Second Street
Grantor:	Assemblies, Inc.
Grantee:	Faith Temple
Legal Description:	Lots 3 through 9, Block 9, and Lots 10 through 12, Block 8, Town Survey
Cash Equivalent Sales Price:	$800,000
Per sq. ft.	$32.00
Per sq. ft. - improvements only:	$30.47
Per seat:	$1,455
Terms:	The reported contract price was $550,000 with an additional trade-in allowance of $250,000 for the Old Temple Church located at 113 W. Gem Road. The $550,000 was cash to the seller. The Old Temple Church was subsequently sold two months later for $250,000 net. This sale appears generally cash equivalent.
Land Area:	1.6 acres or 69,696 sq. ft.
Building Area:	25,000 sq. ft.
Land to Bldg. Ratio:	2.8:1
Sanctuary Seating:	550
Sq. ft. per seat:	45 sq. ft.
Confirmed by:	Phil Mars, broker
Land Description:	This is a level interior site with frontage on Second Street.
Description of Improvements:	This is a sale of three brick buildings with a weighted average age of 35 years. There is an 8,000-sq.-ft. sanctuary (seating for 550 persons) and a 17,000-sq.-ft. two-story education building. Total square footage was reported at 25,000 sq. ft. The overall condition was reported as typical for its age. The seller reportedly expended $150,000 on the education building over the preceding two years. Parking is reported as adequate due to extensive on-street parking in the area. The use is conforming by local zoning. Land value was based on the sale of a site two blocks away last year for $0.55 per sq. ft., and a similar listing for $0.60 per sq. ft. Cost new was based on a national cost service.

Improved Sales Analysis

The sales have been analyzed on the basis of price per square foot. As the comparable sales have a wide range of land-to-building ratios, they have been analyzed on a sale price per square foot of improvements only. The sale prices per square foot, with and without land, are as follows:

Sale	Sale Price/sq. ft. (including land)	Sale Price/sq. ft (improvements only)
1	$78.72	$55.07
2	$42.93	$39.95
3	$38.58	$36.47
4	$32.00	$30.47

The following is a summary of the improved sales, followed by the improved sales analysis.

Sale	Location	Date of Sale	Bldg. Area (sq. ft.)	Seating
1	18 Mill Road	Current	4,700	N/A
2	8809 Kirby	Six months ago	11,000	320
3	7400 Ella	1 year ago	51,454	1,500
4	700 Second Street	2 years ago	25,000	550
Subject	400 West Drive	N/A	10,000	N/A

Your attention is drawn to the following discussion on the adjustments considered appropriate to the sales as compared to the subject.

Conditions of Sale: Sale No. 4 included a trade, which subsequently sold for the price noted in the sale write-up. All costs associated with the trade were further included in the analysis. Therefore, this sale is considered at market and no adjustment for condition of sale was made.

Terms of Sale: The financing terms of the improved comparable sales were analyzed. Sale Nos. 2 and 3 included financing from the sellers. Nonetheless, an analysis of these two sales indicated that they were cash equivalent. Therefore neither was adjusted for cash equivalency. The other sales were considered cash equivalent.

Market Condition Adjustment: The next factor analyzed was market conditions or time. Comparable sales ranged in dates of sale from current to two years ago. Because the market is and has been relatively stable, no adjustment for date of sale or market conditions was noted.

Location Adjustment: Locational attributes of the comparable sales were carefully analyzed in comparison with the subject property. In analyzing each of the sales, the land or site value was deducted. This is necessary to extract depreciation and to adjust for the various land-to-building ratios noted previously. In effect, by removing the land value from each sale, locational attributes are generally accounted for. Therefore, no locational adjustments were considered necessary. It is recognized that improvements in superior locations can contribute more value than similar improvements in inferior locations. Nonetheless, given the relatively similar locations and land values of each of the sales, as well as the fact that land value has been removed from each sale, no location adjustments appear indicated.

Condition/Age: Typically, older religious facilities tend to sell for lower unit prices compared to comparable newer properties in superior condition. This is due to differences in depreciation and/or condition as well as in overall design and appeal.

Given the comparable sales provided here, adjustments for condition/age are indicated. All of the properties are of a similar design and appeal. Therefore, a comparison of the total depreciation for the subject property with that of the sales can provide a reasonable basis for an age/condition adjustment. As this comparison is of *total* depreciation, the adjustment accounts for all forms of depreciation influencing the sales as compared to the subject. This appears reasonable as the depreciation in excess of physical deterioration is similar. The adjustments are based on the following formula:

$$\frac{(1 - \text{depreciation of the subject}) - (1 - \text{depreciation of the sale})}{(1 - \text{depreciation of the sale})}$$

This adjustment could be developed in a variety of ways, yet this tends to compare the sales to the subject based on a "percent good" factor. Each of the sales has been adjusted for condition and age according to this formula, recognizing that depreciation in excess of physical depreciation is being accounted for in this adjustment.

It is recognized that by adjusting for total depreciation, the depreciation in excess of physical depreciation in each sale is adjusted to the subject. As an alternative one could adjust only for physical depreciation and deduct the excess of physical depreciation after the final value conclusion. In the case given here, depreciation in excess of physical depreciation is relatively similar, which situation lends itself well to this analysis.

CONDITION / AGE ADJUSTMENT AS PERCENTAGES

Sale	Indicated Total Depreciation	Estimated Depreciation–Subject	Indicated Adjustment
1	.18	.28	-12%
2	.27	.28	-1%
3	.19	.28	-11%
4	.53	.28	53%

Quality: Quite obviously, religious facilities of better quality will sell for more than those of lesser quality. This is true subject to the law of diminishing returns. That is to say, at a certain point, an improvement for a given market can likely be overimproved. The subject facility is considered to be an average quality improvement. To account for the quality between the sales and the subject, the estimated cost new of the subject has been compared with that of the sales. The difference, as a percentage, provides a basis for developing an adjustment. The derivation of the quality adjustments appears in the following chart. The indicated adjustments are only a benchmark and suggestion for the market.

QUALITY ADJUSTMENTS

Sale	Quality Rating	Estimated Replacement Cost New	Subject Estimated Replacement Cost New	Difference	Indicated Adjustment
1	Good	$67.50 sq. ft.	$71.50 sq. ft.	$4.00	+6%
2	Average	$55.00	$71.50	$16.50	+30%
3	Average minus	$45.00	$71.50	$26.50	+59%
4	Average	$65.00	$71.50	$6.50	+10%

It is suggested that the local market be carefully analyzed to determine if the quality adjustments are reasonable to apply on a direct basis. In some cases this adjustment should be tempered, as buyers are only partially aware of quality differences and might only be willing to pay for a part of the quality available. In this case, for illustration purposes, the adjustment has been left at face value.)

A summary of the adjustments noted herein appears on the following grid.

ADJUSTMENT GRID CHART FOR A RELIGIOUS FACILITY (Sales per Square Foot without Land)

	Sale No. 1	Sale No. 2	Sale No. 3	Sale No. 4
Date of Sale	Current	Six months ago	One year ago	Two years ago
Unadjusted sale price/sq. ft. w/o land	$55.07	$39.95	$36.47	$30.47
Conditions of sale	0.00%	0.00%	0.00%	0.00%
Financing adjustment	0.00%	0.00%	0.00%	0.00%
Adjusted price	$55.07	$39.95	$36.47	$30.47
Time adjustment	0.00%	0.00%	0.00%	0.00%
Adjusted unit price	$55.07	$39.95	$36.47	$30.47
Location adjustment	0.00%	0.00%	0.00%	0.00%
Condition/age adjustment	-12%	-1%	-11%	53%
Quality/feature adjustment	6%	30%	59%	10%
Total adjustment	-6%	29%	48%	63%
Adjusted unit price	$51.77	$51.53	$53.98	$49.67

Conclusion

These adjustments tend to indicate a value for the subject improvements without land from a low of $49.67 to a high of $53.98 per square foot. The total net adjustments to each of the sales range from -6% to 63%. Sale No. 1 has the least adjustments, is the most recent sale, and indicates a value of $51.77 per square foot. Sale No. 2 is the next least adjusted, is a recent sale, is similar in size to that of the subject, and indicates a value of $51.53 per square foot Sale No. 3 had adjustments of 48%, was significantly larger than the subject, and has an indicated value $53.98 per square foot, which is at the upper end of the indicated range. Sale No. 4 is the oldest of the sales, is somewhat larger than the subject, had the largest amount of adjustments, and indicated a value of $49.67 per square foot at the lower end of the range. Given that Sale No. 4 is the oldest of the sales and required the most adjustments, only nominal emphasis was placed on this sale. Reliance was placed on Sale Nos. 1 and 2, with some nominal emphasis on Sale Nos. 3 and 4.

A value estimate of $615,000 appears well supported as follows:

$51.50/sq. ft. x 10,000 sq. ft. = $515,000

Plus land value $100,000

Total: $615,000

Chapter Eight
FINANCING OF
RELIGIOUS FACILITIES

*B*ecause one of the primary uses of an appraisal of a religious facility is often related to financing, this chapter will to help tie the financing function with the valuation methodology. It will cover sources of financing, how lenders view religious facilities, typical underwriting standards, and the loan application process. Insight into the use of the report can be a helpful tool in the valuation process.

LOAN SOURCES

Numerous loan sources exist for religious/nonprofit facilities including banks (local and regional), savings & loans, broker-dealers, REITs, private "hard money" lenders, religious groups, sellers, and individuals.

Banks, particularly those in the local community, are typically very active in the financing of religious facilities. Banks view lending to religious facilities first as a positive function for the community and second as a great source for cross-selling other banking services. In some cases lending to a religious facility located in a certain area may also fulfill the institution's requirements under the Community Reinvestment Act. Religious bodies typically do represent a reliable credit, and bank loans, almost always for "market value," are governed by the requirements of a particular institution, which in turn is regulated by various state and federal guidelines.

Loans to religious facilities from thrift institutions are relatively rare, in part because S&Ls are not as common as in the past and also because they traditionally focused on commercial and single-family lending. However, some S&Ls still hold and originate religious facility loans, operating in today's market in much the same way as a bank that lends to a religious facility.

Broker-dealers are a very active group of lenders who originate, underwrite, and market securities known as "church bonds," which are registered in every state where they expect to be sold. A church bond is a debt instrument secured by the physical facility and is an obligation of the religious body.

These bond lenders, who are typically members of the National Association of Securities Dealers (NASD), usually develop an extensive prospectus on the property in order to register with the various states in which they do business. Bond lenders tend to have more flexibility with respect to the structure of the ultimate financing (loan amounts, rates, terms, etc.) compared to a federally insured bank. Thus, many religious groups needing flexibility will seek bond financing.

This type of financing occurs in two different types of programs. The first program provides the religious facility with a "firm commitment" or firm underwriting for financing similar to a bank's, with requirements for funding (loan-to-value ratios, audited financial statements, etc.). In this program a funding source is established to close the loan before the bonds are sold. Thus, with firm underwriting the loan amount is guaranteed.

The other program, generally referred to as a "best efforts lender program," relies primarily on the members of the religious facility or others to buy the bonds and fund the loan. In effect the members of the facility are financing it themselves. Under this program, the loan amount is not guaranteed but is based on the amount of bonds sold. Funding occurs only if the bonds are sold. Thus, the bond program is undertaken on a "best efforts" basis. Because there is no commitment to fund the entire loan amount, the fees or points are typically less than those for a firm underwriting commitment.

Larger and better capitalized broker-dealers typically provide firm underwriting programs, since they have the capital to fund the loans at closing and before the actual bonds are sold. These programs are generally more expensive than other bond programs and are often used for building programs. The best efforts programs are more typically offered by smaller broker-dealers and are mostly used by smaller facilities.

There are a limited number of real estate investment trusts (REITs) developed to provide financing for religious facilities. This is a new source of capital for religious facility loans and tends to target smaller facilities. There has been some talk on Wall Street currently about the potential securitization of religious facility loans.

Many religious bodies have their own financing arms, developed to finance either new facilities or expansions in their "group." These agencies have underwriting standards and are funded by the main body for the purpose of expanding the number of members and therefore the beliefs of the group. This is oftentimes considered a part of the group's proselytizing effort. Availability of funds can be a function of membership, growth trends, etc. This source of financing is mainly for smaller "start-up" facilities.

In an attempt to expand their influence, some religious groups may finance a splinter group, although this is not very common. The financing source may supply small amounts of funds to keep a small group/facility viable or to help the efforts of a small but growing facility that has beliefs similar to that of the original group/lender.

HOW LENDERS VIEW RELIGIOUS FACILITIES (FEASIBILITY ANALYSIS)

Lenders attempt to view loans to religious facilities from a cash-flow standpoint, which is difficult for appraisers for a variety of issues. The cash flow that lenders focus on is related to collections, and appraisers are generally focused on a rental rate or an income stream generated by the real estate. Dividing the two is generally impossible. Although some religious facilities are leased, this is rare. Where leasing occurs, the lease rates typically are not tied to a market rate but are often a function of numerous externalities. Additionally, because most religious facilities are nonprofit, developing an equity return on the intangible of "religious satisfaction" is subjective at best.

It would appear, therefore, that a formal income approach for a religious facility is inapplicable. Nonetheless, most lenders look carefully at the income and membership side (trends/amounts) of a particular congregation. Normally, as with single-family residences or commercial properties, appraisers would view this as an underwriting issue. Most lenders, however, determine the loan amounts, in part, as a function of cash flow as well as the value of the real estate. As such, it is considered prudent to determine from a general feasibility standpoint if the existing or a typical local congregation could reasonably support the facility being appraised.

The feasibility of a facility for a given congregation is generally tied to several underwriting standards or rules of thumb. These include membership growth/stability, income trends, how income is collected (dues, pledges, tithing, etc.), expenses, leadership, schools, and other factors.

Thus, although not a formal income approach, a feasibility analysis is sometimes applicable to a given congregation. Obviously, if an expansion is occurring, one would expect the need to be driven by an expanding membership. Sometimes this growth is gradual, occurring from family growth. More often than not, growth is tied to population increases in the community (new homes), employment growth, or presence of a charismatic leader (competent management). Items to look for are trends in membership, service attendance, and church school attendance, etc. Viewing the actual membership numbers and knowing how they are developed are imperative to determine if growth is occurring. Most religious facilities keep careful track of their members and maintain attendance figures for worship services and church school. It is not unusual for growing facilities to hold two or more full identical services per worship day to meet the needs of the congregation in the existing facility. Other factors that indicate membership is growing are reflected in the expanding needs of the members. If over a five-year period a facility has worn out the carpet in the sanctuary twice, has had to add temporary buildings (a common situation), and needs additional room for fulfilling the needs of the members, an expansion may be appropriate.

Second, and from a lender's perspective typically the most important, is the trend in income. This is normally viewed over a three- to four-year period. Lenders tend to set their mortgage in part on the income generated by the facility. This is obviously an attempt to develop a loan that the congregation can afford. There are some lenders who view a loan to a religious facility as a cash-flow or business credit loan (i.e., a loan based on the cash flow generated). Obviously, the facility is the focal point of worship, meeting, teaching, etc., and as such, its inclusion in the equation is normally imperative.

A typical underwriting standard tends to indicate a loan equal to what one-third of the discretionary income would support at a market rate and over a reasonable time period given the facility.

Items to consider include the facility's operating budget, additional obligations (other debt, pledges to new churches, etc.), and income from a school, day-care, or elderly care facility, as well as any nondiscretionary income. Nondiscretionary income is related to a gift, pledge, or donation to the facility that is to be applied to a specific item such as a mission, school, or other special-purpose item. Normally, nondiscretionary income is not considered applicable to the loan or debt service. In some cases, however, nondiscretionary income is used to meet expenses such as utilities or landscaping, and as such its inclusion would be appropriate.

Some religious groups have dues, others have obligations relative to members' incomes, and many simply allow members to give as they can or will. Some simply try to convince members to give as much as they comfortably can.

Trying to correlate a congregation's income levels with giving per family unit is often futile due to the propensity of some groups to give more than others. It appears that giving patterns are related to a leader's ability to raise funds and provide a facility that fulfills a real need in the community. As members see the facility providing them with more, they are apt to give more. It is not unusual even for congregations with lower-income members to have similar giving patterns as more affluent congregations, depending on the leadership/management, needs fulfilled, etc.

In most real estate appraisals an assumption that is made is "competent management." A similar concept must be adopted with religious facilities. This factor typically focuses on the facility's board or ruling body. Many religious facilities are governed by a board made up of numerous individuals who are very involved in the facility's operations. Succession of the existing leadership is also a key factor. Different groups look for different types of leaders. A large and charismatic group will need a similarly talented leader. From an appraiser's standpoint, it is important that a reasonably competent leader be in place or is being sought. Some lenders insist on a succession plan in case something happens to the existing leader.

The acceptance of a budget and the process by which it is developed is imperative to the proper operation of the a facility. How a facility spends the dollars that it collects is of importance in that a portion of these funds are expected to pay principal and debt on the facility.

The feasibility analysis developed herein is NOT AN INCOME APPROACH TO VALUE for a religious facility. In theory, it would appear impossible to develop an income approach to value. First, typically there is no profit factor. Second, although religious facilities sometimes rent, at what rate would the income be capitalized? How can an equity dividend rate or discount rate be developed without a profit factor? The feasibility approach looks at the facility from a lender's perspective. Although this analysis is only nominally, if at all, indicative of "value," it does tend to indicate if the facility is operating efficiently based on industry standards. In total, the feasibility approach is a "test of reasonableness" or "sensitivity analysis" of the concluded value by the cost and sales comparison approaches.

A typical income and membership chart coupled with a feasibility analysis follow:

Item	Membership (Giving Units)	Income	Available for Debt Service Monthly	Debt Service supported @ 9.5%/20 years	Value Indication @ 70% LTV
Three years ago	300	$150,000	$4,167	$447,040	$638,629
Two years ago	290	$145,000	$4,028	$423,128	$617,326
Last year	350	$175,000	$4,861	$521,493	$744,990
Year to Date Annualized	375	$185,000	$5,139*	$551,317**	$787,596***

*$185,000/3 (maximum debt service typically allowed)/12 (to get to monthly figures)
** PV supported at a monthly PMT of $5,139, an interest rate of 9.5% and a 20-year amortization.

***Mortgage / .7 loan to value ratio

This chart indicates that the congregation is and has been growing for the last three years. Often this type of data will include an aberrant year (positive or negative) and typically for cause. Either a building campaign was developed, a leader left, or a new one came, etc. The important concept is to note the trends. These data are probably best looked at in the continuum and only as support for the values developed in the cost and sales comparison approaches.

The amount available for debt service has been developed as a function of the total income. Though far from standard, underwriters/lenders of religious facilities often use an amount that is one-third of the total discretionary income as being available for debt service. There are numerous variations on this theme. Some lenders will extend a loan where less than one-third of total discretionary income is available but at a higher loan-to-value ratio. Other lenders will use a higher percentage of the income and agree to a lower loan-to-value ratio.

The amount available for debt service is calculated to support a given amount at market terms. In the example a 20-year, 9.5%, fully amortizing loan is assumed. This figure represents a typical religious facility's ability to repay debt. When queried, lenders differ significantly on the loan-to-value ratio. Nonetheless, a large group uses a range of 65% to 80%. The requirements under this range reflect the lender's comfort with the religious entity and its leaders. Other factors include the amounts allowed for debt service under the previous calculations. That is to say, if only 30% of the facility's income is allowed for debt service, the lender oftentimes will allow a higher loan-to-value ratio.

In the example, a loan-to-value ratio of 70% was used as typical in many markets. Obviously, one would have to query local lenders for their perspective on this issue. A fallacy in this analysis is that the lower the loan-to-value ratio and conceptually, therefore, the less risk in the loan, the higher the value indicated. Conversely, the higher the loan-to-value ratio and conceptually the higher the loan risk, the lower the value indicated. Thus it is imperative to view this analysis only as a benchmark for feasibility based on industry standards that have and will change over time.

In conclusion, this approach/methodology should only be used relative to area/industry standards, and only as a guide to the values developed by the cost and sales comparison approaches.

UNDERWRITING PROCESS

Lenders use a variety of techniques and look for a variety of items in analyzing a religious group. Though not inclusive the following list, noted from different lenders' loan applications, provides a summary of the type of questions asked by many lenders with respect to the "operations" of the facility. Many of the items relate to the facility and actual operations as well as the structure of the borrower, or what an appraiser would refer to as "competent management." As indicated earlier in this chapter, there is a trend among lenders to view a religious facility loan less as a real estate loan and more as a credit risk or cash-flow oriented loan. Other lenders have a difficult time separating the two. Regardless, at present the real estate becomes a crucial element of most all religious facility loans. From a regulatory standpoint, most religious facility loans must be classified as real estate.

Credit/Loan Issues

Purpose:

- refinance?
- new facility?
- new site?
- addition?
- rehabilitation?
- personal property?

Borrower:

- Is the group incorporated?
- Are the articles/documents consistent with the lender's needs?
- Is the nonprofit status in good standing?
- Who has the right to bind the congregation?

- How was/is the loan agreed to by the members?

- Will the loan be approved by the members?

- Will the loan be guaranteed by anyone or a group?

- How is the congregation managed (trustees, board, board of elders, etc.)?

- How old is the congregation?

- What is the denomination?

- Is it a "mainline" denomination?

Facility

- How large is the site—is there room for expansion or additional parking?

- How large is the facility?

- Has the facility ever been appraised?

- What are the physical attributes of the facility (seating, ratio of seating to total area, condition, age, etc.)?

- What is the purpose of the addition or new construction and is it needed?

- If proposed construction or an addition, is it functional for an alternative yet similar user?

- If new construction, have the plans been bid by more than one contractor, are the contractors bondable, and are the contractors associated with the congregation?

- Is there a school and is it state certified?

- Is there a day-care facility that is state certified?

- Is there a nursing home, congregate care, or independent living facility and if so is it state certified?

Leadership/management

- Who is the spiritual leader of the congregation (history of leader, education, years in practice, years with congregation, salary, health)?

- Is there a leader in training?

- Is there a business manager or committee?

- What is the structure of the organization?

- Are the group's legal documents current and available?

- Do these documents require a vote of the membership to bind the congregation?

Financial

- How are funds raised (offerings, weekly giving, stewardship program, pledges, dues, tithes, beneficiary)?

- Is there income from other sources (rent, day care, schools, book stores, restaurants, etc.)?

Some congregations have profit centers that sell information, videos, books, and other data.

- Are any significant pledges or offerings delinquent? Some organizations have large givers that impact significantly on the financials of an organization.

- Is there an ongoing fund-raising program?

- Is there a building fund or drive?

- What are the salaries of the leaders and how are they determined?

- Are there financial controls for collections, in particular for cash?

- Does the congregation have a finance committee?

- Does the congregation have to provide funds to a larger governing body (state, district, national, etc.)?

- Is a school being operated at the facility? If so, how is it funded?

- How is school and/or day care income accounted for? Is it a profit center?

- Are quarterly financials available?

Area Data

- What are trends of the neighborhood (growth, stability, decline)?

- Is the membership drawn from the area?

- Has the congregation existed in the neighborhood for an extended period?

- What service does the facility fulfill in the area and is it likely to change in the near future?

- Are there other facilities nearby that compete for members?

- Are other facilities in the area growing, declining, or stable?

Membership

- How many members are there and how is membership measured?

- What are the demographics of members—families, singles, etc.?

- How many families are considered members and how are they measured?

- How many services are held per week?

- How many members attend services?

- How many children and/or adults attend church school?

The above items were generated from loan application packages from a variety of financial institutions. They are representative of items some lenders consider relevant. Many of these items have only nominal impact on "market value," yet most do tend to have an impact on the viability of the operation. It is therefore important to understand how religious organizations operate in order to accurately determine the value of the facility.

Lenders tend to have rules of thumb by which they operate. Although these "rules" vary, they appear to have their roots in answers to the above questions and the following generalities.

Annual debt service to annual receipts (typically net of building fund drives, as they are typically a one-time giving) and nondiscretionary income should generally not be greater than 30% to 35%. A rule of thumb of 33% is typical in the market.

If there is a building fund, over how many years is it spread and is the giving per member in line with what the congregation is attempting to raise? This shows the lender the members' commitment to the facility.

In general, many lenders feel that the total loan should not exceed two and a half to three times the annual church receipts. Amortization varies greatly from approximately 15 years to 25 or 30 years, depending on the facility and the needs of the religious body. Loan-to-value ratios are generally 65% to 80% with a propensity near 70%.

It is common for congregations to spend all that they take in. Other than savings for buildings and other items, this appears reasonable as they are typically "not for profit."

There tends to be a propensity for lenders to agree to a loan amount supported by the maximum debt service, assuming that 33% or less of the total income (less nondiscretionary income) is used for debt service at current interest rates. Obviously, variations exist with respect to the above. But in general, this appears to be the typical scenario for lenders looking at religious facilities. Lenders with a less than a 33% debt service requirement will often have a higher loan-to-value ratio.

The largest variance noted in financing relates to the flexibility available from various lenders. Banks and other federally insured lenders tend to have a relatively inflexible structure, whereas other lenders have a great deal of flexibility in their structure.

With the current focus on generated "cash flow" in the underwriting of religious facilities, to preserve the cash flow and decrease the risk associated with the same, many lenders have suggested that the leaders sign "noncompetition agreements" or agree to continue on in the capacity for an extended period. Additionally, "key man life insurance policy" requirements are not atypical for leaders of large congregations. Numerous facilities have failed when a dynamic leader has left or formed a splinter group. These underwriting decisions are an effort to reduce the risk of default and, therefore, the quality and quantity of the cash flow.

This chapter is far from covering all aspects of financing of religious facilities. Its intent is to provide a framework for understanding the financing function relative to the valuation process and the feasibility of a given congregation or facility. The issues discussed relative to lender requests for information on a given institution were developed to provide the reader with more insight into the operations of a typical facility and issues that "drive" the congregation.